Brand
To Sell

Vince Ferraro

BRAND TO SELL™

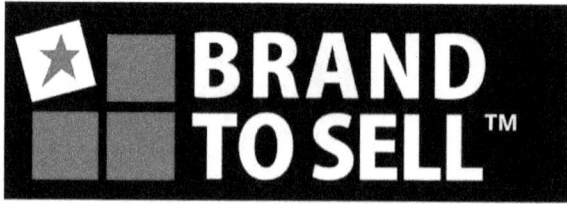

First Edition: November, 15, 2015
ISBN-13: 978-0692613665

Abundant Press
Publish - Promote - Profit - Position - Platform AbundantPress.com

REGISTER

This book for more content

(Audios, Special Reports, etc.)

at:

BrandtoSellBook.com

Acknowledgment

This book has been an idea of mine for the last five years and a serious project for the last two.

As my career has progressed, I wanted to figure out a way to give back to the community by training people in the business and marketing techniques I used to grow multi-billion dollar businesses in Fortune 100 companies. Throughout my career, I have developed some unique perspectives and insights about the business functions of branding and marketing. If I have learned one thing over the last 30 years in the marketing profession, it is that our role in an organization is a complex one—a blend of science and art, with constantly changing tools, methods and processes. There is no one right way to solve a marketing problem and in some ways, marketers must plan in multiple dimensions, assessing every possible scenario and outcome of the brand, product and marketing decisions we make today. The marketing role is not an easy one and it partially explains why the Chief Marketing Officers have some of the highest turnover rates in the C-Suite.

To be successful in any business, you need to have a differentiated brand, loyal customers and be able to deliver exceptional and personalized customer experiences. This book is just the first of a series I have locked up in my brain. In addition, it comes with a corresponding self-paced training program at MyBrandtoSell.com. My goal is to publish additional books and training courses simultaneously.

There is a tremendous ecosystem behind every book and I want to thank my wife Wee-Nah and son Jonathan for giving me the time to think about and write this book. I also want to thank Brian Newton, Andy Broadaway and his team for their book marketing and content editing prowess. In the area of content development and research, I want to thank Michelle (Misha) and the entire staff of Eliseon Marketing.

Finally, I want to thank Hewlett-Packard, Eastman Kodak and Michelin (and their employees) for giving me many of the 'practitioner' experiences and ideas to make this book possible.

Introduction

Welcome to BRAND TO SELL™! It's important that you go through each chapter sequentially, one at a time, as each provides you with a strong foundation for the next chapter of this book. In addition, each chapter contains exercises and links to additional online content. Thank you for reading and I hope you enjoy this book!

Branding Yourself As An Expert

This is the first essential key to branding – showing off your expertise, skills and authority. If you know what you're doing and you're passionate about it and you do it extremely well, then you're nearly halfway there! So what does it take to become an expert? Malcolm Gladwell writes in his book *Outliers* that it takes 10,000 hours (or 10 years) of dedicated and deliberate practice to become an expert – and not just any practice will do. We're talking about the kind of intensive practice that hones and expands your skill to new dimensions.

Other people would point to education, published works (especially in academia) or media visibility being the 'secret sauce' of expert status. While that's true, especially in the lives of Bill Gates and other masters of their craft, often what you need to do is just practice a skill long enough (and diligently enough) to achieve the result you desire. The only problem with this is that many think being 'mediocre' or 'as good as the next guy' is good enough to be labeled an expert.

In today's digital world where information is free and easily accessible by every person (and their 8-year-old child), it's common to know 'just enough' to get by. To be an expert, you need to be better than that; you don't have to be the best, per se, but you do need to offer a reason, perspective or an angle strong enough to put you (and your expertise) in the running as the leader and authority in your field. Hence, while 10 years of deliberate practice may seem intimidating and 20 hours of practice each week may not be enough to set you apart, it all comes down to knowing what level you need to be on in order to excel in your specific field and stand out.

Therefore, the bar for expert status may be higher or lower depending on your industry and profession.

Once you are aware of that, you can start on your path to Mastery and be able to accurately benchmark and track your progress along the way with real measurable milestones and results.

The Back Story

It all started in a small shop right next door to a funeral home, which, with the shop's clever name, caused quite a bit of confusion for the morgue's delivery guy. "Oh no! Where do I take the bodies? The funeral home or The Body Shop?" While the location caused a bit of stir, the shop itself had the odds stacked against it.

After all, it was just another cosmetic business started by yet another stay-at-home mom in her garage. There were hundreds and thousands of competitors already doing the same thing, but only bigger and better (and with a much larger marketing and creation budget). So how would the owner of The Body Shop, Anita Roddick, carve her niche in the over-saturated body and skincare market? She had a vision. She had a determination and drive to succeed and she knew the importance of telling a story. Out of a need for survival, Anita concocted cosmetics from "every little ingredient with a story" that she had stored in her garage. She opened her first shop in Brighton with just 15 products.

But she knew she still needed a hook – a unique story that would set her brand apart. So she based The Body Shop on a unique business philosophy founded on socially responsible principles. Anita wanted her company to offer "a two-for-one sale no other cosmetic company could ever hope to match: buy a bottle of 'natural' lotion and get social justice for free."

From campaigning to save Brazilian rain forests to fighting for fairer trade rules, Anita dedicated her company to social activism both at home and abroad. Part of that powerful brand identity came from putting "Against Animal Testing" on all The Body Shop products, setting them apart from all the rest by reaching out to the hungry and supportive eco and animal-rights niche.

Her focused niche targeting paid off; by 2004, there were over 1,980 Body Shop stores in over 40 countries around the world. It was voted the second most trust brand in the United Kingdom and even earned Anita the highest honor of being knighted by the Queen. The incredible success of The Body Shop led to the opportunity to sell the company to L'Oréal for a cool $104 million. Now that's the power of branding in action. What an amazing turnaround for a garage-business in an already saturated and highly competitive market!

There is no doubt Anita's knowledge and understanding that 'stories sell' is part of what made her successful. She once agreed that stories sell, "… if they are authentic. In every pre-industrial group I have ever traveled and been with, storytelling is the basis of their education. It is about the myths and legends. It's about what makes you divine, what separates you from the rest."

And she couldn't be more right. Your brand's authentic story and public perception is what will make or break your success, regardless of your career or industry. The one thing to remember above all in your brand: You can't please everyone.

And you should never try it.

In this book, I will teach you how to find your perfect audience and niche, build your brand and then market it, but keep in mind that marketing is more for awareness than for gaining business. As we go along in this book, we'll be building a strong foundation and just as with the construction of any building, we'll go step by step, from the ground up, until you have a perfectly crafted and polished brand.

With that thought in mind, what exactly is a brand? Or more aptly, what is YOUR brand? For me, branding is really just a love story between you and what you do and shows the bigger picture of who you really are. It's all about finding the specific people you are meant to serve. It's about improving their lives – not just your own success.

Of course there are hundreds of other interesting definitions and opinions on what a brand is, including:

- The intangible sum of a product's attributes – name, packaging, price, history, reputation and the way it's advertised.

- The essence or promise that a product, service or company will deliver or be experienced by a buyer.

- A 'gut feeling' about a product, service or company.

- Names or symbols that identify the unique source of a product or service.

- The personification or personality of an organization, product or service.

- A single concept or idea created and embedded in the mind of the customer.

- A name, sign or symbol used to identify items or services of the seller(s) and to differentiate them from goods of competitors.

- A set of associations that enhance or detract from the related product or service.

- A unique value proposition that sets you apart.

- A collection of perceptions created and embedded in the mind of the consumer through marketing, persuasion and storytelling.

- A way to succinctly show your authority and expertise in a particular niche or industry and spread the message of who you are and what you're about.

- A brand can be a product, service, company or person with something to offer and 'sell' that will benefit others in some way.

All of these are great and reflect various aspects of a brand, but my own personal favorite is from Ze Frank of Buzzfeed because it's a bit more colorful and descriptive:

"A brand is an emotional aftertaste that's conjured up by, but not necessarily dependent on, a series of experiences. If you leverage those aftertastes, people will pay attention."

I think it's a brilliant quote that sums up the essence and the entire point of branding: What effect will you have? What emotional aftertaste will you leave – on everyone that comes in contact with you, your services, your products, your name and your unique personality?

What is the total experience and impression you want your clients, customers and fans to have when they leave your office, see your presentation or visit your store?

Will they know what you stand for and believe in? Will they know who you are and why you do what you do? Will they know—with just one glance—what you can do for them to make their lives better, richer and more fulfilling?

The key here is to create the exact 'aftertaste' or experience you want your customers to have. Don't leave it to chance. Using a coffee metaphor, that could run the gamut from mild to a dark roast espresso of a brand and everything in between. That's what this entire book is all about.

But what's incredible is how few people are actively pursuing and creating a brand for themselves right now—less than 1%—which means you have the advantage and the upper hand over your competition by starting my S.T.A.R.™ Branding Process right now.

As I mentioned earlier, in this book I'll be taking you step by step through the entire process of branding, from understanding and leveraging your strengths and weaknesses and defining/refining your brand, to creatively marketing your brand throughout the world. This is all in the context of creating the set of experiences, impressions and the overall aftertaste you want people to have when they come in contact with your brand.

The reason I've created this book is because I want you and/or your company to be the best brand it can possibly be. In order to do this, I will provide you with a blueprint for success—a system I developed and honed after building and managing some of the most successful and iconic brands in the world.

I believe anyone can follow this road map and build a successful, forward-leaning, differentiated brand.

Having said that, I must also warn you ...

This requires your personal effort and energy, as well as help from a coach or friends, if you know people you can trust to give you honest feedback. This is not a "get rich quick program" that promises that you will make $100K in 100 days.

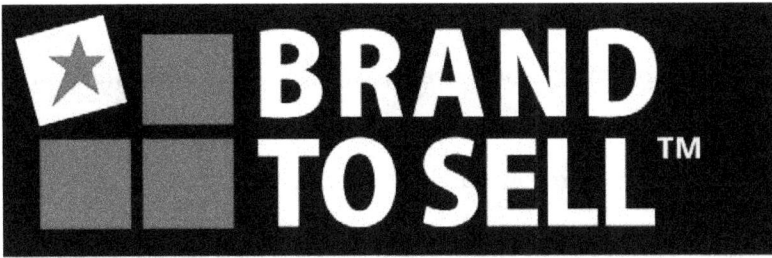

Table Of Contents

CHAPTER 4

Reputation And Total Management Of Your Brand

REGISTER
This book for more content
(Audios, Special Reports, etc.)
at:
BrandtoSellBook.com

About The Author

The Creator of the SuperS.T.A.R.™ BRAND TO SELL™ Course

"Vince is an energetic leader and marketer who inspires his teams to deliver results, but still enjoys doing it. He isn't afraid to take risks and think unconventionally. He has a passion for doing what is right for the customer while delivering innovative products that help meet the needs of the marketplace."

– Mark Gehrett, Worldwide Product Marketing Manager, LaserJets, Hewlett Packard

With more than three decades of career experience in global business management and marketing, Vince Ferraro has overseen a variety of iconic consumer and B2B brands and businesses. From Fortune 100 companies to entrepreneurial start-ups. His successes include strategic brand management, product development and marketing leadership results within hardware, software and solutions markets.

As Executive Vice President & CMO for digital hardware and marketing services start-up Attenditus Networks, Vince is currently charged with day-to-day marketing operations, fostering critical mass of its application-rich, interactive touchscreen solutions for kiosks and digital display advertising markets.

He was previously VP of Global Marketing for Kodak's Consumer Digital Group and Corporate Marketing, while providing marketing leadership to Kodak's Consumer Business (digital cameras, video cameras, film products, kiosks and ink jet printers). He also served as Global VP of Marketing for its Commercial Printing business.

In his 26 years with Hewlett-Packard, Vince ran marketing for some of the world's most successful technology products: PaintJet, DeskJet, OfficeJet, PhotoSmart and LaserJet. He also helmed Global Marketing for HP's iconic LaserJet business unit and oversaw its Business and Imaging Group and Consumer Businesses in various marketing management and finance roles.

He continues to author the popular blog VincentFerraro.com and is the co-author of the best-selling book, *In it To Win It: Strategies for Winning in Business and Life*. Vince also consults with and sits on advisory boards in nonprofit organizations, established businesses and incubator start-ups to increase the effectiveness of their business strategies and marketing plans.

He earned an MBA from the W.P. Carey School of Business at Arizona State University and is a graduate of Stanford University's Strategic Marketing Management Program.

Visit his websites at VincentFerraro.com or the MyBrandtoSell.com training website.

What Does the S.T.A.R.™ In SuperS.T.A.R.™ Mean?

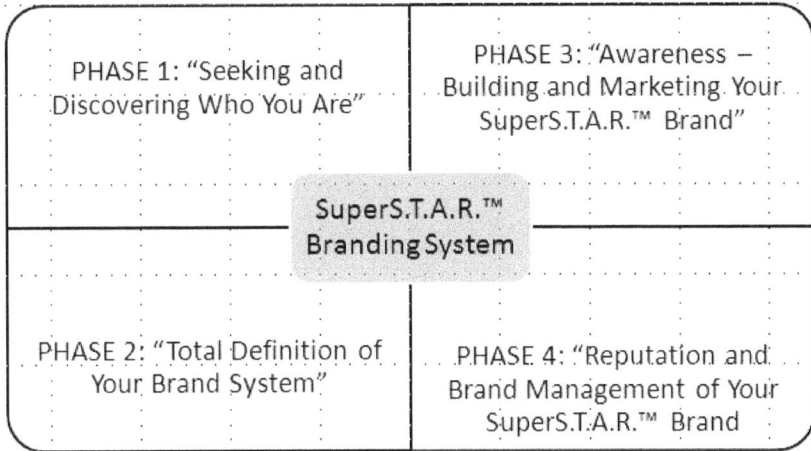

PHASE 1: "Seeking and Discovering Who You Are"	PHASE 3: "Awareness – Building and Marketing Your SuperS.T.A.R.™ Brand"
SuperS.T.A.R.™ Branding System	
PHASE 2: "Total Definition of Your Brand System"	PHASE 4: "Reputation and Brand Management of Your SuperS.T.A.R.™ Brand

Phase1:

Seeking to Discover Who You Are

Phase2:

Total Definition of Your Brand System

Phase3:

Awareness Building and Marketing Your SuperS.T.A.R.™ Brand"

Phase4:

Reputation and Brand Management of Your SuperS.T.A.R.™ Brand"

I've set this book up in such a way that when you finish reading and complete the supplemental online exercises, you'll be empowered with all the skills, knowledge, research and understanding needed to discover, create and market your own powerful, magnetic and authentic personal brand.

I have also included some bonus content that you can download for free by registering at: MyBrandtoSellBook.com. So what are you waiting for?

Let's get started!

SuperS.T.A.R.™ Branding: Will It Work For Me?

We all know celebrities rarely brand on their own. They have agents, publicists and managers to help set up product endorsement deals, make connections, get air time and interviews and generally help them stay in the public eye as much as possible. But then there are those rare celebs that go a step further – all on their own.

Maybe they spend their days campaigning for a charity or cause or start their own fashion line. Maybe they go on a diet and suddenly become the face of the newest weight loss program or supplement. Whatever it is, these celebs seem to have the inside track on how to really create and sell a brand in a way that brings in fame and fortune. But they are celebrities ... the rest of us aren't.

So how does this translate over to all of us?

Well first things first – we are ALL stars at something. Maybe you have a unique talent or skill, vast knowledge or experience in a particular niche, an incredible ability to inspire or motivate or maybe you're just phenomenally good at one or two specific things.

Once you pinpoint what that is and start to define and refine it (like I will teach you in the coming chapters), then branding like a star isn't all that difficult. Sure, you may not have an agent or publicist to get you multi-million dollar deals with Nike or Chanel, but you will have the knowledge, skills and experience to help get you to "Super-Star Status" in your niche for your own brand.

I'll go into all of that in much more detail coming up. For now, let's just look at a few things popular celebrity brands all seem to have in common that help to make their personal branding efforts a success. Keep in mind it's not what YOU think about you or your brand, it's what OTHERS think about you! Here is a list:

- Master your craft. Don't be mediocre at a lot of things. Instead, focus on being really good at one or two and make that what you're known for.

- Be known for something, but make sure it's what you really want!

- Build or shape an ideology, lifestyle or story around your brand.

- Leverage what you have to offer, no matter what that may be.

- When and if it feels right, turn your personal brand into a business and cash in.

- Be congruent! If your message, values, etc. don't match your brand, don't do it.

- Be an interesting person and inspire others in some way.

- Be human, real, approachable, authentic and attainable ... within reason. (unless your angle is all about being exclusive and arrogant, of course).

- Listen to what your audience wants, what it asks for and what it's interested in (and leverage it to your advantage!).

- Be a great storyteller and draw your fans and audience into an experience; take them on a journey with you and they will connect with you on a very deep level.

- Evolve, grow and expand – avoid becoming stale and predictable.

- LOVE YOUR FANS – reward them, make them feel special, elite, exclusive and wanted. Lady Gaga and her Little Monsters are one great example.

- Diversify your brand investments (think Kim Kardashian and Donald Trump). Once you have an established brand, you will want to tap its equity to drive new businesses, products and services.

- Use social media to build and spread your brand like your life depended on it (since your brand's life actually does!). THIS is how the celebs are doing it – and it's working like crazy!

- Get a tough skin! You're not going to please everyone (and that's not the goal) with your brand every time and on everything!

- Controversy, negative publicity and extreme branding doesn't work for everyone (unless you're Charlie Sheen ... WINNING!).

Just be sure to keep these things in mind as you are creating, refining and marketing your brand over the next few weeks and months, as they are absolutely essential to your personal branding success!

A Brief, But Essential
History Lesson In Branding

To really grasp the evolution and purpose of today's style of branding, you need to get a glimpse of how it came about.

Often, what comes to mind when someone says 'branding' is the old cowboy way of marking cattle with a hot iron to let everyone know which steers belonged to whom. In fact, the word brand actually comes from the Norse word brandr, meaning 'to burn.'

But 'branding' goes back much further than that, even if wasn't known by that particular word.

Before spoken and written languages were common, people used images to correlate with specific thoughts or actions.

Later on, as the world became more civilized, merchants from Egypt, India, China, Rome and Greece used pictures and symbols in place of words on their signs so that those who could not read would know what was being sold in the shop.

But branding (as we know it) didn't really come into its own until the late 1800's when the economic boom meant people had more discretionary income to spend on wants and whims, instead of just basic survival needs.

With the increasing level of income, more products and services were being offered and the market was soon flooded with so many choices and competitors that businesses and entertainers were forced to find new ways to differentiate themselves and stand out. Instead of using images and names to identify what was inside or where it came from, merchants began using brands to create stories, elicit desire and create a sense of exclusivity and expertise.

Think of clothes (Levi's), tobacco (Marlboro), soft drinks (Coca Cola), tires (Michelin) and beer (Budweiser) leading the charge in the early days of branding. To see what I mean, take a look at this great Brand Evolution Timeline:

Brand Evolution Timeline

Now you can see where our ideas of branding came from and how they play into what we think about branding and marketing today. But it's gone even beyond just an image or way of standing out. It's so much more now.

We've become so interconnected and social, so outspoken and sensitive to hype, that we demand more from our companies and public figures.

We demand transparency, engagement and authenticity. We demand expertise and authority.

We demand stellar service, outstanding performance and a deeper connection and rapport with those we choose to buy from. Most of all, we demand outrageously unique experiences, the kind that leave us breathless from wonder and excitement—something we can write home about, brag to our family and friends and use as part of our own identities.

That's what real branding is about – creating unique experiences that anchor positive and powerful emotions in the minds and hearts of your market and link them to using your products or services or even just being around you.

But before you can start creating your brand, you need to identify and demonstrate your expertise, give customers a reason to trust you, listen to what they have to say and then connect the dots. That's where becoming an expert comes into play.

Branding Yourself As An Expert

This is the first essential key to branding – showing off your expertise, skills and authority. If you know what you're doing, you're passionate about it and you do it extremely well, then you're nearly halfway there!

Personal vs. Company Branding

I get this question all the time from my clients and it can be a perplexing problem for them, especially if they are not the owner of the company or if they are the owner but also have several other companies.

The answer is actually pretty simple and straightforward – both. But you should always build your personal brand first. Always.

Because a personal brand will always stay with you, even when you move to a different company or start a new one. If you're an employee looking to climb the corporate ladder or a skilled talent looking for the perfect job, a powerful personal brand is what will help you land that coveted spot in the company of your dreams by setting you apart from all the other applicants.

While there are people out there who would say you can't be a good corporate employee and build a personal brand at the same time because it is too self-serving, I don't agree.

You already have a brand at work. The only question is this. Is it positive, negative or indifferent? You may not be managing it well. Knowing this is key to your success.

If you're a small business owner or a professional practitioner, your personal brand is even more important because people don't buy from companies – they buy from people.

Have you noticed how consumers will either boycott a company or passionately support it, all because of something the owner believes in or stands for?

Think about the recent uproar over Chick-Fil-A's public stance on gay rights. Whatever side you're on, you've probably made a choice to either support or boycott that company based solely on the outspoken views and clear 'brand' of the owner ... no matter how you feel about their chicken tenders and waffle fries.

Another example of personal branding affecting a company's brand is the recent statement by Abercrombie & Fitch CEO, Mike Jeffries. When he stated his company purposely made clothes in small and medium sizes only because they didn't want "unattractive and unpopular" people wearing and promoting the brand, it caused a backlash that went viral overnight. The backlash included protesting in front of Abercrombie & Fitch and Hollister stores, a rash of homeless wearing secondhand Abercrombie clothes and a drop in overall sales and share prices. In both of these cases, the owners' personal brand and company brand collided and become inseparable, even if that wasn't their original intention.

The same goes if you're a one-man-show and even more so.

A personal brand is all you have if you're an author, public speaker, entertainer, musician or politician. You are the company, the product, the service and the brand, all rolled into one. For example, I bet you can name at least one musician or actor that you vehemently despise and you refuse to watch or listen to anything by them, all because of something they said, did or supported.

Whether driven by politics, religion, morality or just plain stupidity, their personal brand left you with an unpleasant aftertaste and you no longer wanted to have anything to do with them, despite their talent or popularity.

That's why your personal brand and your company brand (if you have one), should always be congruent.

It's the power of authenticity and it's absolutely necessary – unless you purposely keep something hidden that doesn't match with your brand (which is difficult to do in this day and age). Which brings me to my next point – how will branding yourself (and your company) make your life better?

CHAPTER

1

Seeking to Discover Who You Are

"You will recognize your own path when you come upon it, because you will suddenly have all the energy and imagination you will ever need." **– Jerry Gillies**

"Be yourself; everyone else is already taken." **– Oscar Wilde**

In Alice and Wonderland, Lewis Carroll says, "Who in the world am I? Ah, that's the great puzzle." That is appropriate because in order to brand yourself or your business appropriately, it requires patience and an understanding of who you are as a person, what you value, what you do well, what you do poorly and so on and so forth. This knowledge comes from not only what you are today but who you want to be in the future.

It is not just about you in a job, business or professional context. It will also include elements of who you are (and want to become) as parent, son/daughter, sibling, co-worker, Little League coach or church elder. You are you! You are distinct and quite unique to anybody else on this planet. If you better understand yourself and what makes you different from other people, you can use that knowledge to create an unfair advantage in your occupation or work.

Listen. We all have things we are great in and some things in which we don't do so well. Most if not all of us have been in jobs that did not match our skill sets or interests. I am the first to admit that. When I was transitioning in the summer for graduate school in the 1980s, I had the opportunity to work at a local bank branch as a teller.

This was before computers and everything was a manual process. Of all the tellers, I was probably the one that was short or over my balance more often at the end of the day. Fortunately, I left that job to go to graduate school after a few stressful months. I was not good in this job and I knew it!

When I started my corporate career at HP, I started out as a cost accountant and financial analyst. This was a great job for any newly-minted MBA and I relished the opportunity to learn the business through a financial lens.

But I really wanted to be a marketing person—a Product Marketing Engineer as they called us in those days—because I always had a passion for people, customers, solving problems and creating ideas for new products. I was "good enough" for the financial role to be promoted to a manager with conversations about me being on the "controller track" for my next career move.

While anybody who wanted a career in finance would have been delighted with the career progression and promotional track I was on, I made my share of mistakes in counting inventory, costing existing products and pricing new ones. I eventually found the right path sneaking into a forecasting/analyst role and eventually becoming VP of Marketing for several multi-billion dollar printing and imaging businesses at Hewlett-Packard.

In fact, being a marketing executive with a background in finance was a value wedge for me and differentiated me from most marketing people who were engineers or were art history majors before they were marketers.

I found my path after careful consideration of what I did well and what I did poorly, what I liked and disliked and what I thought was the best utilization of the skill sets I brought to my employer.

Finally, I found something I could get motivated to wake up to and feel inspired to accomplish. Although I am no Mother Theresa, I still feel like I have touched millions of people who bought and were satisfied with the printers my team and I created. To this day, it energizes and inspires me to create new products and businesses!

In addition, the creative process requires introspection and occasionally, some tough love – mostly directed at yourself! It also requires a lot of honesty.

But I deeply believe that if you apply the principles and techniques outlined in this book, there is a high likelihood that you will dramatically increase your income potential no matter what your occupation or profession is. If you build your brand properly, it will carry with you into the future, regardless of your present job or profession.

I know you can do this, so let's get right to it!

What Makes A SuperS.T.A.R.™ Brand?

Ah, this is the answer we all want and need to hear. Is it having a massive marketing budget or a team of quirky hipster advertising agents plotting brand anarchy? Nope.

It's nowhere near that complicated or expensive. In fact, having a SuperS.T.A.R. ™ Brand all comes down to you and only you. What I mean is that it's up to you to create your own brand from the inside out. Of course I will help you (at every step) as your branding Sherpa and guide.

To do that, you need to understand a few things about what makes a brand truly iconic—what gives it personality and staying-power to outlast all the other fly-by-night brands that come and go each year. Think about Coca-Cola and how it's outlasted so many other brands of soft drinks in the past century. Think about the causes it's stood behind and the fondness you feel when you hear the song "I'd Like to Teach the World to Sing." That's the kind of iconic brand you want to create. If a sugary soft drink can do it, then with a little time, passion, determination, clarity and effort, so can you! I like this Venn diagram, by Ryan Morse, that explains how a number of elements come together to create a kick-ass brand.

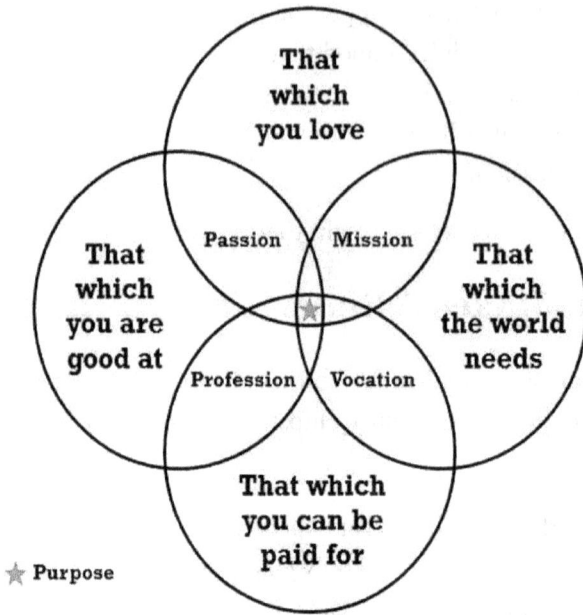

Source: https://twitter.com/ryanmorse33/status/469934009594957824/
photo/1

Ideally, a great brand comes from the intersection of these four areas and becomes the foundation of your brand.

- Doing what you love (passion, energy, mission).

- Doing what you are good at (expertise, profession).

- Doing what you can get paid for (people will pay, perceived value).

- Doing what the world needs (user need, market demand).

Hopefully, you have some of all four elements. But if you don't, you must pick one of these orientations and drive that element in your value wedge. It is essential that you pick a space where you have the passion, skill and energy to brand. It may be a profession, small business, career shift, etc. Why? Because branding is a mindset as much as it is a strategy. If you don't have the mindset, it will be a lot harder to build a kick-ass brand.

So What Ingredients Need to Come Together In Order To Make the Perfect SuperS.T.A.R. ™ Brand?

Do you want a brand recipe? Let's take a look ...

A SuperS.T.A.R. ™ Brand Definition:

- Taps into the values and ideals of society or a specific subgroup or niche and even has the power and influence to shift those values in a new direction. For example, Whole Foods reaches out to the affluent eco-conscious and organic health-minded market, while a brand like Patek-Philippe embodies a "just because I can" kind of extravagance with $500,000 watches.

- Is derived from or tells a compelling, convincing and memorable story that rings true in the hearts and minds of the target audience. It can be based on its own (or traditional) mythology and legend, a slightly embellished version of the truth, an archetype such as "The Hero's Journey" or a "rags to riches" theme (more about this in a later chapter) or even the pure and simple truth – if it's exciting and relevant enough to be remembered and repeated. Ben & Jerry's is a great example of this, as is Tony Robbins and Madonna.

- Has an image, icon, symbol or emotional essence that makes it instantly recognizable and memorable. You'd know those golden arches from anywhere wouldn't you?

- Can charge premium pricing for the value of the products and services they offer. In addition, clients and customers are attracted to you as you have "lead magnet" capabilities of pulling in demand as opposed to finding and chasing sales.

- Creates a rabid and ravenous following or fan base that promotes the brand on their own because they love it so much and are willing to fight those who speak out against the brand. Think MAC users versus PC users; a MAC user will fight you to the death to defend why MAC is better than a PC.

- Is congruent, synergistic and consistent across the board. Your social profiles and statuses, your website and mission statement, your personal voice, your style and image, your personality, your marketing and promotional material, your recorded and printed statements, your core brand story – everything all has to match and share the same essence, meaning and message. It needs to be the same message your audience is crying out.

- Trustworthy. Brands become great brands because they can be trusted and relied upon. Keep in mind that trust has to be earned over time and if it's ever lost, it's nearly impossible to get back.

- Authentic. What does that mean? Simply put, be who you are, stand for what you truly stand for and be passionate because you can be no other way but passionate. Don't put on a front or pretend to support something just to get paid, for publicity or to build a name. This lack of authenticity and transparency is what we hate about politicians, so why would we trust a brand that does this? One thing we need to remember is that part of being authentic and transparent is that we are human and we make mistakes.

- It's okay if your brand (or even you) isn't perfect. Flaws can be endearing and triumph over troubles can be inspiring. So put a positive spin on anything less than perfect and push it to the forefront with good press.

- Be addictive. A brand should create an emotional (or even physical) attachment and a raging desire to have more and more. It should incite action (such as buying more, telling others about it, passing it around, etc.).

- Provides incredible value and makes the audience/customer's life better and more fulfilled. Fill a void, solve a problem or scratch an itch. If your brand fills a vacuum left by something, then you'll never run out of customers or fans. In fact, one recent study found that companies that aren't making a difference in the world or the individual lives of the consumer are ultimately going to fall into nothingness and cease to exist. It's no longer about making a good product or beating your competition; it's about creating a powerful impact that changes things and people for the better.

- Clear focus. You can't be all things to all people, so choose the one area you are passionate about or skilled in and make that the focus of your brand. Don't be a "Jack of all trades, master of none."

- A unique promise that you can keep. A unique value proposition you can deliver.

  For example:

  GE: "We Bring Good Things to Life"
  Coke: "Open Happiness"
  Budweiser: "King of Beers"
  Campbell's: "M'm! M'm! Good!"
  FedEx: "When it absolutely, positively has to be there overnight"
  BMW: "The Ultimate Driving Machine"
  Burger King: "Have it your way"

- Commitment and patience. A brand isn't born or grown overnight. It's nurtured and carefully tended over time. Don't get impatient or set yourself up for failure and disappointment with irrational expectations.

- Patience is key to this process and commitment is what will keep you in the branding game long after most others have given up.

Now that you know what a SuperS.T.A.R. ™ Brand looks like and what it is – do you have what it takes to become one? Now, I know this is a bit of a loaded question because I truly believe everyone can build their unique brand with a little effort and focus. That's what this book is all about. What I mean is that there are specific components that go into a successful and iconic brand and you must have each one of these to reach your goal of a SuperS.T.A.R. ™ Brand.

If you're not feeling overly confident right now, it's okay. By the end of this book you will be enlightened, encouraged and empowered with the knowledge and processes you'll need to create an iconic and lasting brand to be proud of! So let's get right into the meat with step two and start digging deep to unearth your true and authentic brand.

Before we go any further, I want to let you know that these next steps (as well as several other steps in this process) contain questions and thinking exercises that are absolutely essential in unearthing your true and authentic S.T.A.R. ™

Brand. They are not optional and you can't just read them and answer them in your head.

Clarity rarely comes that way – you have to work for it.

What Is Your Market Niche?

If you've ever dipped your foot in the internet or consumer marketing waters, then you'll be familiar with the term 'niche.' But if not, let me take a moment to explain it to you.

Simply put, a niche is a marketplace or target audience. It's one specific section or group of people that are most likely to buy or need your product/service and where you direct your marketing attention.

What a niche is NOT, is your ideal client. They are NOT the same thing. Very rarely will you make money by attempting to sell your brand to the entire niche with the same message.

You break it down even further to find the exact group of people that meet all your requirements for being your 'ideal client.'

Actually, I like to think of it like this ...

A niche is like a pond. Within that pond is a variety of fish. Maybe you have some trout, some bass, minnows, goldfish, brim, catfish, a few snakes, bunch of frogs and a handful of turtles.

While your niche may be the entire pond (as compared to a huge lake, a river or the ocean), you wouldn't dream of using the same bait to catch every single kind of fish, nor would you want to catch every kind of fish and animal in that lake.

If your goal is a backyard fish fry for your family, you wouldn't go after the little fish with hardly any meat and you probably wouldn't be interested in the frogs, snakes and turtles. In that case, your ideal fish would be the bass, trout and catfish. Now, if you're having a 'catfish fry,' then obviously only catfish will do and only the full-size adult ones have enough meat, so your focus is now on only one species and size of fish.

Once you know which fish you're after, you can research and get to know the habits of that fish – what do they eat, what attracts them, what scares them away, when do they bite, where do they hide, do they swim in groups, what method works best, etc. All of these things are extremely important to catching that catfish.

This is the best example of a niche and an ideal client that I can think of and it really helps explain how it works. It should not come as a surprise, but if you have found a niche and have expertise in that niche, your chances of being perceived as an expert (in that area) are higher.

That's really good to know when you're considering taking a $5000 full page add out in the Photographic Equipment Collector Weekly magazine.

Now, if you research further, you'll also learn that the photography niche is split into further focused segments – such as professional, amateur, hobbyist, tourist, prosumer, consumer and moms who want adorable pictures of their kids without paying a professional to do it (but need more than their iPhone and Instagram).

If you break the photography niche up even further, you'll see those segments have their own segments.

Professionals include wedding, architecture and scenic, high speed and sports, glamour and boudoir, wildlife and nature, portrait, modeling and head shots, product and food and of course fashion and celebrity, just to name a few.

Some cameras and lenses work great for indoor portraits but are terrible for nature or high speed. If you don't know your ideal client within your niche, then you will never have the success you desire for your brand.

It's just like using a fly fishing bait on a pond to catch trout, but not even knowing it's trout you're actually after and that you're using bait they couldn't care less about!

It just doesn't make sense.

Yet so many marketers and advertisers do this exact thing. Just throw some bait in the water and hope they catch something good. Most of the time, they catch nothing at all ... or maybe an old boot or a turtle. What good is that?

So that's why when it comes to niches, you need to understand that your marketplace—your target audience—may NOT be your ideal client.

But if you don't take the time to research and put forth the effort to find out who your ideal client is and get to know them intimately, then you'll never achieve the level of success for you and your brand that you crave. You'll just be throwing money away on bait that doesn't work and not knowing why or how to fix it.

But I Don't Have A Niche

Actually, you do.

Even if you are a professional looking to brand yourself and get hired or change your career, you have a niche. Your niche is the career/industry you are in and your ideal client is the CEO or hiring manager of the company(s) to which you're applying.

If you're a mom-and-pop store, your niche or target audience will be your town and your ideal client will be those who are nearby, have money and a way to get to you and want/need what you have to sell. If you're a speaker, author, artist or entertainer, your niche is the group of people that would be most interested in what you are saying or creating – and your ideal client would be the person who passionately collects your style of art, listens to speakers in your industry or reads books on your topic and has the disposable money to spend.

You don't have to sell a product or service to have a niche – but if you are selling anything at all, including yourself or your brand, then your ideal client will always be the person or persona of a group of buyers that you are selling to. Pure and simple!

What Makes A Good Niche?

This is a great question and while there are plenty of answers and advice on this topic, I'm going to give you the simplest answer possible ...

A great niche – and the perfect client within that niche – is one where these three things combine to create a perfect storm of success:

1. They are PASSIONATE, even obsessed, with the topic. (Think golfers, surfers, fishing enthusiasts, NASCAR fans, self-improvement fanatics, people looking to lose weight, bodybuilders, etc.) They literally wake up each day thinking of ways to make more money so they can buy more stuff to feed their passion or improve their game.

2. They have the disposable income to spend on products and services and they spend it often! Go to any serious golfer's house and you will find thousands and thousands of dollars in equipment, clothes, how-to books and DVDs, etc. A niche is not a place where people admire but do not buy.

3. They are easy to find, reach and access. If your market isn't consistently and actively online, then you need to know how to reach them. What will be effective marketing – radio, TV, print, direct mail, email marketing, social media and articles, networking and referrals, etc.? If they are online, where do they congregate – online forums and blogs, e-zines, social media, etc.? The cost to acquire leads and clients needs to be factored in if you have the opportunity to choose a niche, such as with internet marketers and online entrepreneurs.

Finding the right customer is paramount. It's what finding a good niche is all about; however, you also need to make sure you can make money in that niche as well.

A great niche is not all about just finding the right target. It's also about finding the "sweet spot" of the niche that you can monetize.

Think about it this way; you want to find the intersection of a niche where there is great demand, low competition and high income potential.

Identifying the Ideal Client Or Customer In Your Niche

When building and refining your brand and bringing it to your audience, your ultimate goal should be to build such a deep and thorough connection and understanding of your customers/clients, that you know beyond a shadow of a doubt where they are now (point A) and where they want to be (point B).

This is your job as a brand leader and it's an important one, because once you know the point A and point B for your target audience, you can then begin to shape your offer and your brand to become the ideal 'expressway' between the two points.

You want to get your customer to their dream outcome in the shortest, easiest, fastest, simplest and most desirable way possible, then be able to tell/show them (through a story, testimonial, case study, USP, value proposition, etc.) precisely how your product, service, talent, company or brand can get them from point A to point B in the fastest, easiest, cheapest, simplest, shortest, most exciting, creative way possible.

It's about you identifying their problem, then making them aware of their problem, agitating the problem and pain so it becomes urgent and critical for them to find a solution, then YOU (your brand) becomes THE BEST (preferably ONLY) solution to that problem of which you have made them painfully aware exists. The key point here is that your offer must truly provide an answer or solution of high quality and value – or you're taking their money and lying to them. This is the LAST thing you want to do with your brand.

Here's a great example:

Take eHarmony.com – they know finding the perfect mate is nearly impossible and their mantra is why waste time with duds when you can find the man or woman of your dreams in a nice clean and scientific way? It makes perfect sense, right? It's almost like placing an order. Once you sign up, they ask you a bazillion weird and highly personal questions that when you answer honestly and objectively, helps to create a profile of your ideal partner.

This is simply brilliant and by their success rate of happy marriages and partnerships, it works. So why not use that same scientific approach when looking for your own ideal client?

What you do is literally create a profile or buyer persona of the client you desire most to work with on a daily basis or the perfect customer you want to have buy from you, by answering a series of detailed and in-depth questions about your ideal client.

So How Do You Do That?

Well, it's going to take a little bit of effort, but let me tell you that if you do this right, your success is practically assured. If you know your ideal client inside and out, you'll make money – even if your product or service isn't that unique and even if your marketing copy sucks. Of course you don't want your marketing to suck and your product/service to be lame, but it just goes to show you that when you find out how to tap into the minds and hearts of your clients, anything is possible.

There are a few ways to get this data, research and info:

1.) Read everything you can get your hands on about and for the niche/ industry you're in. For example, if you are marketing to chefs, you would want to read multiple magazines, articles, websites, blogs and forums, on chefs to find out who they are, what they want, what they need and what problems they are having. Is there a Chefs Monthly magazine you can pick up at Barnes and Noble? Can you join in on some of the forums and online communities where chefs congregate to talk about their industry and passion? Find these places and zero in on them – join right in and start asking questions!

2.) If there is a particular person in your town that you would LOVE to have as a client (or would love a client similar to them), then go and meet with them! Ask them if you can pick their brain over dinner (you're buying) and find out what makes them tick. DO NOT sell them on you, just get info and do research. This is mandatory! After you've done one, do the same for another four or five just like them until you have a small pool of info and data you can cull through to find the similarities they all share.

3.) If you already have a customer database, call them up. Tell them you will give them a gift certificate or a free service/product if they would answer a few questions that will help improve your service/ product. Get as many as you can and start making a list of what they all have in common. Whatever you do, avoid doing this by email or online survey. No one pays attention to these things and they have no human element or interaction, so you won't get the honest and true in-depth answers you're looking for. You do NOT want the generic surface answers everyone spouts off on auto-pilot. You want to be able to ask clarifying questions and get more details and examples and the only way you can do that is in person. So stay away from electronic polls and surveys if you want real, honest data you can actually use.

4.) Pay the big bucks and hire a research team, set up a focus group or purchase an online industry statistics report. This is pricey ($400 - $5000) depending on what you choose), but if this is a long-term business and your livelihood is at stake, then it might just be a necessary investment.

5.) Pay attention to the negative feedback you have received in the past. This is something that most people avoid and the effects of doing that can be devastating to your success and growth. Bill Gates famously once said, "Your most unhappy customers are your greatest source of learning." This statement is so true, but do you know who your unhappy customers are? Do you know what they need? Do you know how to fix their problems and use their criticism to improve and expand to new levels of success?

If you do this right, your end result will be a killer profile similar to eHarmony's dating profile, where you are intimately connected to and are aware of what your ideal clientele wants, needs and expects. Then you can cater to your market to draw them in and give it to them in a way that makes both you and your clients thrilled and fulfilled.

See what a difference that makes? It's not just a difference in how much money you make but also in how much you love your business and love your clients.

If you realize this is your problem—that the clients you're attracting are not the clients you really want—then it's time to step back and analyze your marketing tactics, the words you use to draw your clients in, where you're marketing and your niche.

Understanding Your Business Model

This section focuses on making sure you understand your business model. Simply stated, Investopedia defines a business model as:

"The plan implemented by a company to generate revenue and make a profit from operations. The model includes the components and functions of the business, as well as the revenues it generates and the expenses it incurs."

How important are business models? Professor David Teece of the University of California, Berkeley, once said, "Get the business model wrong and there is almost no chance of success ...". Another way to look at a business model is a diagram that shows all the flows between your company and its customer. It describes the rationale of how an organization creates, delivers and captures value.

Business models are constantly in motion, innovating and changing all of the time. What worked this year may not work in three to five years. Therefore, you need to reevaluate and update your model on an ongoing basis as your competition, goals, skills and brand evolve and grow.

To help give you a better idea, here are a few examples:

Borders Bookstore

The popular bookstore chain, Borders, went out of business after digital delivery and online competition from Amazon sucked the business out of their retail stores. As a retail player in printed books, it failed to recognize/respond to the trends until it was too late. These trends would have significantly impacted their business model, which would have required fewer stores and more of their business online. Eventually Borders went out of business trying to redefine itself as something bigger than a bricks and mortar business. But it was too little too late. Consider Barnes and Noble (in the same business as Borders) who more quickly reacted to these changes, purchased Nook and evolved their retail format to embrace technology, digital delivery, tablets and e-readers. They are still around and considered a market leader in the online and retail book industries.

Dell Computers

In the 1980's, Michael Dell decided to manufacture "build-to-order" custom PCs using the telephone (and later the web). He started out building his PCs in a college dormitory and offering excellent quality at better prices. Back then this was unheard of and was radically different from how HP, Compaq and IBM were building fixed sku inventory for all of their products. Dell and Gateway (another build-to-order PC manufacturer) became household names in the industry and it was hard to find someone without the signature cow-print brand in their home or office!

Business Model Canvas

If you want a metaphor, here is one. The way an overall business model can be thought of as a canvas upon which the business model is painted and made up of these components.

BUSINESS MODEL CANVAS				
KEY PARTNERS	KEY ACTIVITIES	VALUE PROPOSITION	CUSTOMER RELATIONSHIPS	CUSTOMER SEGMENTS
	KEY RESOURCES	What is the bundle of benefits offered?	CHANNELS Customer touch points that play an important role in the customer experience	
COST STRUCTURE			REVENUE STREAMS	

Source: Business Model Generation, Alexander Osterwalder and Yves Pigneur, 2010 http://business.usi.edu/dean/2011spr-cob.aspx

The canvas of the business model needs to weave together some of the following elements in a way that can systematically and predictively make money. These elements include a series of building blocks which describe:

1. The product
2. Customers/users
3. Demand creation
4. Motivations/problems
5. Budget/resources
6. Flows of value and many other things

Business models come in a variety of flavors and sizes that can be used for brick-and-mortar and online businesses. For tangible products and services, here are a few popular examples:

- HP sells printers at a low price and makes money on the recurring revenue that comes from inkjet and toner cartridges, warranty support and service. It is a similar strategy to Gillette's razor and razor blade model.

- Airline business models are evolving by charging for bags and requiring payment for internet access, meals and movies on board planes. In addition, they dynamically price empty seats to make sure their planes are fully loaded, even if that means the person next to you paid much less than you.

- Kickstarter.com – community funding of extraordinary projects that allows people to reach out to the masses and community to fund their dreams and projects, instead of trying to get traditional grants, bank loans or bootstrapping funding. They charge a commission for the funds they help you raise.

There are many other models out there, especially in the internet space. Famous examples include Priceline (name your price), daily deals (Groupon, Living Social), large format "everything" stores like Walmart, Costco and Staples that sell online and in store.

The following links highlight many more business models that can be used. It's important to note that many businesses have or are evolving to a hybrid model which contains both online and offline business model elements.

They are often described a "bricks and clicks" businesses and many traditional businesses have migrated in this direction by necessity.

Check these resources for more info:

Online Models:

http://thenextweb.com/entrepreneur/2011/05/25/the-9-types-of-online-business-models- which-one-do-you-use/

Offline Models:

http://smallbusiness.chron.com/list-business-models-338.html

One way to help you in your planning is to use this template that helps you collect your thoughts. I would create my own, but I think the document below, by Alexander Osterwalder, works very well for this section's exercise:

http://www.businessmodelgeneration.com/downloads/business_model_canvas_poster.pdf

Analyzing Your Competition

Now that you know your niche, ideal client and how to make money, it's time to find out a little more about your competitors. By competitors I mean people competing against you for the same job, as well as other people in your industry trying to sell their products and services to your marketplace.

So when you see the word 'competitor' and you learn how to understand them, find their weaknesses and strengths, keep in mind how it relates to you and how you can shape your analysis of them to match your own specific needs.

Before I go into the best way to analyze your competition, I want to share a personal insight with you, because after all, this entire system is about finding your own uniqueness and branding it – not copying your competition.

Doing a complete competitor analysis is a great way to get inspired in both opportunities and ideas, but many use it incorrectly. They look to find what their competition is doing and then try to copy it or make their own offerings bigger and more elaborate so they can compete on the same level. This is the old paradigm, the obsolete way of running your business.

In today's world where networking and partnership are highly valued and often more successful than campaigning against your competition to bring them down; you need to open your mind to a new way of thinking.

It's not about how you can beat your competition anymore. It's about how you can create a place for yourself where there are no competitors because only you do what you do, in the way you do it.

This is also referred to as the "customer experience." Delivering on the total product solution in a way your competitors would have a difficult time duplicating.

For example, Jeff Dunham, the well-known and hilariously popular ventriloquist comedian, is worth 45 million dollars and has no other competition because only he has the incredibly delightful Peanut, Walter, Bubba, Jose Jalapeño (on a stick) and Achmed. Only he can produce the style of comedy he's known for and while there are plenty of up-and-coming and old school ventriloquists, only Jeff has made it cool while making millions out of talking to himself. It was his passion and he worked hard to brand himself and it paid off tremendously!

My point is, analyzing your competitors can give you inspiration and show you weaknesses or gaps in the market, but ultimately it comes down to finding out what your own strengths are and using those to your advantage to stand out so far above your competition that no one else can even come close.

One last thing to be careful of is that it's easy to get trapped in the competitive way of thinking—a 'keeping up with the Joneses' mentality—where everything your competitor is doing, you feel like you have to do as well.

If you're not naturally inspired or excited to do it, this can lead you off of your own unique path and into a cookie-cutter-just-like-everyone-else rut and you lose everything that made you special and desirable.

This is exactly how business owners wake up 20 years down the road: miserable, drained and totally burnt out. If you're following your passion, branding yourself or your business in a way that showcases your uniqueness and special assets, then it actually energizes you, fills you with joy, delights customers and gives meaning and purpose to your life. Yes it can also make you tons of money. If you're just trying to compete with everyone else and 'level the playing field' then you will likely end up a bitter, jaded and unfulfilled husk of a person, left wondering how you got so far off track from your dreams and aspirations.

That being said, I do think competitor analysis is essential in getting to know what else is out there and helping you differentiate yourself from everybody else.

One major way that knowing your competitor inside and out and is beneficial to your businesses is when you're engaging in online marketing and increasing your exposure. If you learn where your competitor is advertising, who they are targeting and what keywords they are using to spread the word online, you can make sure you are doing everything you possibly can to rank higher in the search engines and get as much, if not more exposure (and the business) than they are getting.

How To Use S.W.O.T. Analysis To Understand Your Competition

There is a popular and very concise way of getting to know your competitors called the SWOT method. It stands for "Strengths, Weaknesses, Opportunities and Threats" and it gives you an easy way to find out what your competition is doing and how well they're doing it.

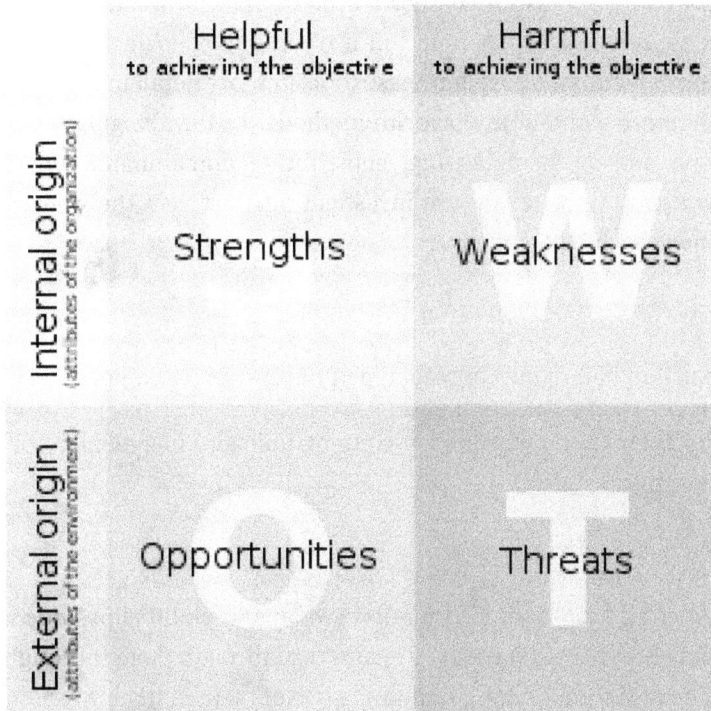

	Helpful to achieving the objective	Harmful to achieving the objective
Internal origin (attributes of the organization)	Strengths	Weaknesses
External origin (attributes of the environment)	Opportunities	Threats

Source: https://commons.wikimedia.org/wiki/File:SWOT_en.svg

Of course, before you start you'll need to do some research on your competition so you have the necessary data to complete the competitive analysis. There are many ways to do this and here are just a few:

- Visit your competitors' websites and read their sales and product literature, check out their product selection and prices, look at their images and read their FAQs. Come at it from a customer's viewpoint; what would you be looking for and concerned with if you were a first time customer considering a purchase from them?

- Use advanced Google search techniques to find hidden content on the web. Did you know that websites can keep information invisible by preventing the major search engines from indexing certain types of content when doing a search? I can show you some techniques to identify some of this content. Please note, this is not hacking. We are not using passwords to hack a system. Instead we are finding hidden content that was not found in a traditional Google search. I have an entire handout to explain these tools in more detail in my training site. Here are some of my favorite methods. In the Google search engine, type one of the following, substituting domainname.com with the company website you are investigating. Just visit the websites below and see what you uncover:

indexof:domainname.com/

inurl:domainname.com/ filetype:pdf (or docx, xlsx, pptx)

inurl:domainname.com/wp-content/uploads/ filetype:pdf (or docx, xlsx, pptx)

insite:domainname.com/

- Download any free information (webinars, audio clips, videos, books and ebooks) they have to offer and read through them thoroughly. Take note of the quality, accuracy and style of their content.

- Sign up for any ezines, newsletters or email notices from them so you can stay in the inner circle and get all the new info right as it comes out.

- Purchase one or all of their products (or services) and analyze them so you can get firsthand experience of what it's like to own and use their products. Look for any flaws, weaknesses, strengths or gaps in the way the products work or run.

- Call their customer support line to get a feeling for how they handle customer issues.

- Look at how they are marketing and branding themselves. Do they have a core brand story? How is the audience responding to it? Have they gone viral on social media? Where are they advertising? What are they saying? Are they using the same message for everyone or are they niche marketing? What is their USP and value proposition? How are they packaging, bundling and presenting their product or service?

- Go to http://www.SEMRush.com and sign up for an account. This will give you access to your competitors' search engine ranking, Adwords account and keyword information – which is invaluable to your own marketing.

- Check public records for patents pending, trademarks and copyrights (to see what they're thinking about doing next) and also public records for info on market share, company value, press releases, yearly reports, customer reviews and testimonials, statistics, databases, major clients, vendors, affiliates and resellers or other important data, etc.

- If your competitors have brick-and-mortar stores, you can visit (as a customer) or if they are entertainers/speakers/public figures and you can go see them live, then definitely do so. And be sure to ask other viewers or customers what they think of the competitor while you're there. This kind of casual feedback can be invaluable helping you formulate your own strategies.

- Who is their audience and who is their ideal client? How does it differ from yours?

Self-Assessment And Your Personal S.W.O.T.

Now that you know pretty much everything there is to know about your competitors, it's time to evaluate who YOU are and where you are as a brand.

What are your strengths? Where are you weak? Are there opportunities you're giving away to others or missing internally? Are there internal threats that if left unattended could destroy your brand or business from the inside out? Any external threats you need to be aware of?

The Personal S.W.O.T. Analysis works exactly the same way as the competitor one except YOU are the focal point. If you're a job-seeker or career-changer, then you would find your own personal strengths, weaknesses, opportunities and threats. If you're an entrepreneur, professional, small business owner or company CEO, then you would do the S.W.O.T. on your company's, employees, your brand's strengths, weaknesses, opportunities and internal/external threats.

Doing your personal or brand SWOT is extremely important as it gives you a starting-off snapshot of where you are now, shows you the direction you need to go in and what to focus on changing, improving and enhancing in order to be successful.

As I mentioned earlier, S.W.O.T. stands for strengths, weaknesses, opportunities and threats. But what does that really mean?

Let's break it down before you start your own SWOT profile:

- **Strengths:** What are you doing right? Where are you finding success? Do you have an online chat support system? Satisfaction guarantee? A killer customer service? Awesome rewards and incentive program? Is your product or service totally unique and 100% effective? Are you successfully using social media to promote your brand?

- **Weaknesses:** What are your shortcomings and flaws? Is your email response rate slow or non-existent? Are there multiple negative reviews or complaints about how your product or service works? Are you paying too much for leads and eating into your profits and you know you can do better? Is your copy weak and self-serving instead of benefit-driven? Have you lost any market share, major clients or important vendors? Do you have a limited marketing budget or knowledge of SEO and how social media works? Find out your specific weaknesses so you can avoid falling into the same traps and also improve on them.

- **Opportunities:** During your search into your weaknesses, did you find anything that you can do to fill a void or gap in the market (such as targeting a specific group they may not be targeting) or can you fix a flaw in your design or use their weaknesses to improve upon your own product or service? If so, these are your opportunities for growth; take them. With some creative thought and dedicated effort, your weaknesses can become your strengths!

- **Threats:** If your competitors are succeeding and growing at alarming rates and their customers seem happy, then this can be seen as a potential threat to you. Find out why they are growing and flourishing so you can get ideas and inspiration on growing your own brand in your own way. Another threat could be up-and-coming companies or people that have a product, service or brand similar to yours. It's been said that every time one person has an idea, at least a dozen others have the same idea and the winner is the one who gets it out to the public first with the best marketing execution. When you create a successful product, the copycats and knock-offs are only a few steps behind.

Keep in mind that you don't necessarily have to compete directly with your competitors in order to succeed. Often times, it is not advisable to do that; however, you can make it big by offering something memorable or just being unique in an appealing way.

Chapter Two is all about finding your own uniqueness, value proposition, core branding story and powerful selling points, so don't get discouraged if you feel you can't compete on their level yet. With a little time and effort, you can surpass them and become your own icon of success.

One final thing. It will be tempting to fall into the trap of getting defensive and even jealous while you're analyzing your competition. You may feel that urge to lash out, sabotage or just react emotionally toward your competition.

Whatever you do, stay calm and stay in control. If you act irrationally and get defensive, you're playing their game on their terms, instead of your own game on your own terms.

You'll never find true success or happiness that way.

Remember that branding is about telling your customer and ideal client what's in it for them and how you, your product or your service can enhance and improve their lives in some positive way.

If you get too stuck on crushing your competition, copying their actions or competing on their level, you'll lose sight of this and then nothing you do will matter, because without your clients, you have nothing!

REGISTER

This book for more content

(Videos, Special Reports, etc.)

at:

BrandtoSellBook.com

CHAPTER
2
Total Development of Your Brand

"All of us need to understand the importance of branding. We are CEOs of our own companies: Me Inc. To be in business today, our most important job is to be head marketer for the brand called You." – **Tom Peters in Fast Company**

"Building a brand is a lot like building a house. You have to lay the foundation first. The frame, plumbing, wiring, the roof, cabinets, window coverings all have a unique role and are important elements in making that house not only strong but attractive and livable." – **Vince Ferraro**

When I was a kid, I liked to build stuff. My neighborhood gang—Dave, Danny and all of the others—used to devise all sorts of schemes to create something from nothing. A go cart from an old pallet, a house made of a discarded water heater box, a fort made from the side of the sofa and blanket and homemade fireworks. We were an ingenious lot. We took the materials we had available and we were limited only by our imagination.

Architects learn the same way, at least some of them. At Taliesin West, the Frank Lloyd Wright School of Architecture in Scottsdale, Arizona, their Student Shelter program is a unique experiential learning opportunity for students to design, build and live in a structure they have created while enrolled at Taliesin.

They are given a 10 sq. ft. concrete slab and various construction elements like tarps, wood, support poles, as part of the "learning by doing" educational approach advocated by Frank Lloyd Wright. The program demonstrates how climate, building materials, site orientation and client needs and preferences inform design choices based on the tenets of Wright's organic architecture.

Constructing a shelter engages a student fully in a process of architectural discovery, where inspiration and hard work are joined with fellowship and commitment.

Building a brand is a lot like building a house. You have to lay the foundation first. The frame, plumbing, wiring, the roof, cabinets and window coverings all have a unique role and are important elements in making that house not only strong but attractive and livable. A house with a wall or roof missing is not a home; it is a shell, a decayed structure or worse, a pile of wood and construction materials that used to be a house.

Whether you choose do it yourself, with someone or hire somebody to do it for you, you need to have an architect's mindset to build or enhance your brand – whether it be you, your company or professional business. All the elements need to come together in a unique way which fits who you are as a person. A house with a weak wall or roof would be unstable. So too would be a weak brand without a strong value proposition or visual identity.

This chapter is all about building your brand's structure. There are 12 key elements to build you brand's architecture. It goes way beyond a logo to include your brand's vision, mission, values, personality, key messages and much more.

Defining Your Brand Vision, Mission And BHAG

In this chapter, we're going to dig deep into the lifeblood of your brand – your vision, your offer, your unique selling point and your core brand story.

This can't be done in your head and it can't be done in an hour. If you think you can, then you're doing it wrong or you're not putting your heart and soul into it. You have to dig deep and it takes time to peel the layers back one by one to find the core truth hidden beneath.

Branding Requires A Plan, Just Like Running a Business Or Building A Home

So how important is defining your brand down to the very last detail?

Let me give you an example ...

You walk into an architect's office with your vision of a brand new dream home swimming in your head. You tell him you're ready to build and he says *"Fantastic! What kind of home do you want?"*

"The one I've been dreaming of since I was a little kid. Tons of rooms, lots of space, really cool," you say. And the architect replies, *"Ok, that's a good start – what else?"*

You stare blankly back at him because that's as far as you've gotten in planning your dream home. He frowns and tells you to come back when you have a detailed plan on everything you want. He needs to know how big, how many rooms and bathrooms, what architectural style – all the way down to the color and type of tiles on your bathroom wall and where you want your electrical outlets to be located.

Just like you can't go into an architect's office with only a fuzzy inkling of a home design in your head and expect to walk out happy, you can't go into branding without total clarity in every aspect of your business, offer, message and your brand itself.

So that's why this next Phase is THE most important set of steps during your branding journey. So sit back, pay attention and enjoy the ride to the inner depths of your soul – where the core of your brand lies.

You've often heard the phrase *"Without a vision the people will perish"* and this is truer than you know. In fact, here are a few statistics to prove my point:

1. **A Harvard University Study that was done** across businesses in 20 industries showed that companies with vision statements saw their revenue grow more than four times faster; job creation was seven times higher; their stock price grew 12 times faster; and profit performance was 750% higher. Wow!

2. **Newsweek** looked at 1000 companies with vision statements and found that an average return on stockholder equity was 16.1%, while companies without them had only a 7.9% average return. That's less than half!

3. **"Built to Last"** showed that for companies with vision vtatements, a $1 investment in 1926 would have returned $6,350 compared to only a return of $950 for comparable companies without a Vision.

Those are some pretty powerful and very interesting stats that should go a long way in showing you the power and necessity of having a clear vision.

Does Having A Vision Statement Pay Off?

Yes. Yes it does.

As you can see from the stats above, companies that have clear and concise brand visions have a better sense of who they are, where they are going, what it takes to get there and they know when they have arrived. They know how to tell if an opportunity or course of action is right for them by running it against their brand vision to see if it matches and enhances what they stand for and where they are going.

> One great example of having a clear vision that actually came to pass was when Henry Ford said, *"I will build a motor car for the great multitude ... It will be so low in price that no man making a good salary will be unable to own one and enjoy with his family the blessing of hours of pleasure in God's great open spaces ... When I'm through, everybody will be able to afford one and everyone will have one. The horse will have disappeared from our highways, the automobile will be taken for granted [and we will] give a large number of men employment at good wages."*

Look around you today and you'll see that Ford's vision came true. That's the power of a clear brand vision statement; knowing where you're going so you can create a road map of business steps to take to get you there.

Envision Your Future With BHAGs

Another part of the brand vision process is to create and build a future for yourself and your brand that you want to experience 10 to 30 years down the road.

I'm not talking about normal day-to-day monthly or yearly goals that every company or individual develops. What I mean is the 'big picture' of what you want to accomplish. The reason you exist, the purpose for getting up and continuing to work. These are called BHAGs.

What are BHAGs? A BHAG (pronounced BEE-hag) is a Big Hairy Audacious Goal that you use as your focal point—your end goal—and it is what you use to run every decision and opportunity against to see if it's in line with achieving this goal.

BHAG is a term first coined by James Collins and Jerry Porras in their 1994 book titled, *Built to Last: Successful Habits of Visionary Companies*. It is a powerful guidance system and motivating statement that rallies your team and your fans behind accomplishing a single focused goal.

In fact, a true BHAG *forces* you to become a visionary by looking so far into the future that you often end up changing and adapting your current paradigm or way of thinking in order to meet your goal. If you know that you cannot reach that goal in a year or even five in the way you are doing things now, then you bring about a change so revolutionary that a change is imminent if you stay on the right path – and your BHAG was the catalyst that caused that positive change.

Without it you would never have known where to start to begin the change or that a change was even needed.

To understand this idea a bit better, let's look at the BHAG's of a few major companies and compare their current progress and success against their vision statement:

> **Amazon** - "Every book, ever printed, in any language, all available in less than 60 seconds."

Disney - "Be the best company in the world for all fields of family entertainment."

Ford - "Democratize the automobile."

Google - "Organize the world's information and make it universally accessible and useful."

Microsoft - "A computer on every desk and in every home."

Most of these companies have either accomplished their BHAG already or they are well on their way. And I can guarantee you that without this clearly laid out vision to guide them along the way, they would have faltered, strayed off the path and not reached their intended goal.

Many would have gone bankrupt from mis-spending money or going after things that did not help them move closer to their BHAG.

Vision vs. Mission

I have found that there is often confusion between a vision and mission. Let me explain the difference. Both these things serve different purposes for a company/brand but are often confused with each other, even among Fortune 100 companies! So here is my simple explanation:

*A brand's mission statement describes what the brand wants to experience or create **right now**. A brand's vision statement, on the other hand, depicts what the brand wants to be in the **future**.*

A mission statement talks about HOW you will get to where you want to be (vision) and the steps you are taking to get there. In contrast, a vision statement shows your end result – the "WHERE" in your journey. It also weaves in the values and purpose of your brand and always speaks in future tense to what you aspire to be and will achieve.

Here is a quick example:

In a famous 1961 speech, John F. Kennedy said this about the space program:

> "I believe that this nation should commit itself to achieving the goal, before this decade is out, of landing a man on the Moon and returning

him safely to the Earth." In 1962, he also said "We choose to go to the moon in this decade and do the other things, not because they are easy, but because they are hard, because that goal will serve to organize and measure the best of our energies and skills, because that challenge is one that we are willing to accept, one we are unwilling to postpone and one which we intend to win and the others, too."

This was a huge goal backed by a powerful vision and the challenge was taken on, embraced and achieved through the Gemini and Apollo projects (the how). Man landed on the moon in 1969 and it's now a common thing to go into space. That's also another trait of your vision. Specifically, once it is achieved it becomes commonplace.

What Are You Branding?

Before we start digging, I want to answer one of the most common questions out there: *"what can I (or should I) brand?"*

The answer is "pretty much anything!" But I would not recommend that you brand everything because that would lead to a value proposition that is too broad. The reality is if you want to brand it, you can. Whether it's an umbrella company, your name, professional practice, small business, brick-and-mortar storefront, franchise, product or line of products, service, a division or department, an organization, country, town, a specific talent or skill or even a person, personality or mascot — it can be successfully branded if you go about it the right way.

Do You Have An Irresistible And Deeply Desirable Offer?

Another huge part of your brand is your offer – whatever you are putting up 'for sale', whether for money, support or a fan following or to the general public. Basically your offer is your solution to the problem, pain or need your ideal customer and niche are facing. It can be a product, service, skill, talent, knowledge and expertise or simply a message you want others to hear and adopt.

Simply put, your offer is whatever you want your audience to *buy from you* or *buy into*.

When I say 'buy' I mean that your offer is paid for with either money (which is the most common payment) or with your audience's investment of time, attention, energy or emotional support. That's why your offer could be a message about minimizing our carbon footprint and your ideal clients would be those who pay for your offer with their support emotionally, verbally, physically as well as monetarily. Or it could just as easily be a tangible item such as line of makeup for those with facial scars and your ideal customer pays directly in cash. If you are looking for a job or changing careers, your offer is yourself-everything about you, including what makes you unique and all the passion, talents, skills, education and experience that make you a worthy and desirable candidate for the position.

You may already have an offer in mind or you may be in the process of deciding what you want to put out there as your offer. Either way, there is a nifty little process that can help you define and refine your offer and make sure it's tantalizing and enticing to your ideal customer.

This method is actually called "the 4Ps" and was originally thought up by E. J. McCarthy to help refine the different kinds of choices you have to make in the whole process of bringing an offer to your market.

The 4Ps of Marketing are:

      a.   Product (*or service, skill, message, etc.*)

      b.   Place (*where is your market congregating and buying?*)

      c.   Price (*gives you a profit and gives value to customers*)

      d.   Promotion (*how will you advertise and distribute?*)

There are many other P's out there that people might throw out to you as part of an extended 4P model (5P, 7P). For example, like purpose, people and processes as part of a broader model proposed by others. In this section and exercise, I chose to focus on the 4P's. Why? Because I think the rest are derived from these core four. There are two other models that are often used to create a product offer and they are pretty good tools. One is called the 'whole product solution' that was promoted by Geoffrey A. Moore, in his book *Crossing the Chasm*. The other is the Value Proposition Canvas template, developed by Peter Thomson. The Value Proposition   Canvas makes explicit how you are creating value for your customers. It helps you to design products and services your customers want.

Brand Values – What Do You Stand For?

"Mass advertising can help build brands, but authenticity is what makes them last. If people believe they share values with a company, they will stay loyal to the brand. Authentic brands don't emerge from marketing cubicles or advertising agencies. They emanate from everything the company does ..."

— Howard Schultz, "Pour Your Heart into It: How Starbucks Built a Company One Cup at a Time"

In this book I talk about 'values' a lot – the value of your offer, the value of your brand, the value your customer places on your offer or brand, etc. But the value I think is most important is your own personal set of core values.

What Are Core Values?

Good question ...

Every day in our lives and in our business we make choices. Some are 'easy' and seem to come naturally, while some are more difficult and we have to think about them for a while before we make our decision. Quite often, we think we're making each decision 'in the moment' based on the situation and the facts in front of us, but the truth is ... we're not.

Whether we realize it or not, our choices and decisions are based on our own personal values that we hold dear, rather than any other external influence. These core values are the beliefs, attitudes and judgments we prize and are what dictates how we live our lives in every area and aspect.

In fact, our success and happiness often lies in the order and priority of our core values – what's most important to us. For example, if comfort and safety are high on your list of core values, while adventure and risk-taking are low on your list, then you may decide to pass up an opportunity to buy shares in a new emerging company ... and if that company happened to have been Apple or Microsoft over 30 years ago, then you would have lost out on millions, even billions of dollars.

Even if you bought a share more recently, you would have had a good return because a share today is worth over 40 times its value seven years ago. On the other hand, had that opportunity been one of those dotcoms that popped up overnight and failed within months, you would have made a wise decision in passing on that risk.

Either way, your values are what would have shaped that decision and led you along the path that closely aligned with what you believed to be true, among others in your life like religion, school, politics, career choices and whom you might marry.

It's clear that values drive your life, but as we have all seen in our lives, it's not always a good thing to have your values <u>steering</u> your life, especially when you don't know what they are, how you got them and if they're still even useful and wanted in your life!

That's why in this chapter, I want to help you find your values so you can see what's driving your life and how it's affecting your success and happiness on every level.

If you are an owner of a company or desire to have one, you'll want to make sure your values are well articulated and that they can be described and communicated to your customers, employees, stakeholders, etc.

One way to do it right is by having something so appealing and crave-worthy that it practically starts branding itself.

So What Do My Personal Values Have To Do With Branding?

Everything ...

Your brand is an extension of you. What you stand for, your brand stands for. What you believe in, your brand believes in. Some people will see what your brand stands for and believes in, check to see if *they* believe in the same thing and then choose to buy from you (or not), based solely on whether or not your values match theirs.

Knowing your values is crucial to your success; in fact, here are 10 reasons why knowing your values and prioritizing them in a way that benefits you can help lead you almost effortlessly to success:

1. **Inspiration** – living an inspired life only happens when you know your values and are perfectly aligned with them.

2. **Motivation** – when we fight against our values we become depressed, uninspired and demotivated. Nothing is fun and suddenly our energy just disappears. But when you are clear on your values and you know you are living them, natural energy just seems to bubble from within.

3. **Follow the Right Path** – knowing what you value makes it easier to recognize the opportunities that will ultimately lead you to your goal and you'll never find yourself wondering "how did I end up here?" It's like a GPS so you'll always know you're not on track when you feel discomfort, unease or see red flags; then you can get turned around and get back on track before it's too late.

4. **Crystal Clear Clarity** – you know what you stand for, why you stand for it and why you do what you do. There is no greater power and motivator than clarity.

5. **Authenticity** – being one with your values allows you to live a truly authentic and transparent life. You are who you say you are and congruence is one of the rarest yet most desirable traits in a person and a brand.

6. **Better Time Management** – how you invest and manage your time is directly related to how successful you are, so if you can streamline it and make it more effective by choosing to do only what is of value to you and your happiness, why wouldn't you?

7. **Rekindle the Fire** – bring back your passion for what you do and for life in general by getting to know your value system intimately and living by it ruthlessly!

8. **Make Better Decisions** – we all weigh the pros and cons of every decision in our heads before we make our choice, but if we knew what meant the most to us and what we valued it above all else, our choices would be easier, simpler and less prone to regret.

9. **More Success and Money** – how much more successful would you be if you woke up every morning totally in love with your work? How much more inspired would you be and how many more creative million-dollar ideas would suddenly flow into your brain if you were doing what you truly loved in life?

10. **Your Path is Clear** – when you are aligned with your values and you run everything you do in support of them, the path to your destination is clear. You know what goals to set along the way, what to avoid, who to follow and who to bring with you. It literally answers almost every question you could ask, from "what should I have for lunch today" to "should I partner with this billion-dollar firm?"

The funny thing about values is that even if you don't know where they came from or why you have them, you'll often fight to the death to defend them. After all, they are part of your identity. They make up who you are. And the key here is that your brand's values are an extension of your personal values. They are your brand's identity and make it what it is. So in order to be in control of what your brand stands for and the message your brand is spreading, you need to be aware and in control of what your values are and how they are expressed in your brand.

As you can see, knowing your current values will help you understand why you do what you do and help you make the best choices for you and your brand's success. In fact, I believe that brand values are expressed in every aspect of the business, for example: the products, services, packaging, labor practices and environmental initiatives.

SuperS.T.A.R.™ Brand Clarity Assessment And Self-Audit

Now that you have a clear idea of your brand vision, your own unique offer and your core values, it's time to move on to building your unique selling and value proposition and your brand core story.

But you're not quite ready ... *not yet.*

There's one more exercise to go through to help you prepare and find the clarity you will need for the upcoming sections.

Why Is Clarity So Important?

"It's a lack of clarity that creates chaos and frustration. Those emotions are poison to any living goal. A lack of clarity could put the brakes on any journey to success." — **Steve Maraboli, "Life, the Truth and Being Free"**

Clarity is achieved when a brand has clearness of appearance, thought and style. In addition, it is aligned with reality. Without clarity, your brand is like a rudderless ship lost in a sea of potentials, possibilities and opportunities.

While every direction can take you to a new experience, it might not be the experience you want to have.

If you just sit there rudderless — floating and drifting — hoping the waves and ripples will take you to where the city of gold lies, you might find yourself shipwrecked on a desert island in the middle of nowhere surrounded by hungry sharks.

While this analogy isn't a pleasant one to ponder, I've seen this exact outcome all too often in both experienced businesses and new start-ups full of hopes and dreams. They know the general direction they want to go in (success, money, fame, etc.) but they lack the clarity that allows them to chart an exact course to get them there. I can't tell you how many have come to me asking, "How did I end up like this? I'm so far off from where I wanted and expected to be!"

One of the main reasons for their failure to find success is that they never stop to ask themselves questions such as "how long do I want to take to get there?" or "who/what will I need with me on this journey to help me succeed?"

They sound simple, but it's questions like these that help you define and refine your purpose, vision, goal, offer and your overall brand into a clear and precise course for action that when followed, will lead you right to your desired destination of success by the shortest and easiest path possible.

True clarity comes from asking yourself tough questions that require you to search externally and dig deep internally in order to find the answers you're looking for.

In the end, we want clarity to achieve our version of success as quickly and easily as possible so we can sit back and enjoy the fruits of our labor for the rest of our lives.

Building A Powerful And Seductive USP, Value Proposition And Positioning Statement

Ah, "USP" - if you've ever worked in the internet marketing area, then you have an inkling of what this means ...

Your "USP" is actually your Unique Selling Proposition (or Point) and the phrase was actually coined by dissecting successful ad campaigns from the 1940's and finding what worked. Essentially a USP is a phrase that promises your customers if they buy your product, they will get this specific benefit in return ... something unique to your product, service or brand that no one else has or can say about their offer.

Now, a USP is **not** the same thing as an elevator pitch and I'll explain why.

An elevator pitch (like ones used in career search or networking) is a quick 30- to 60-second summary of your business, service, product, brand or yourself and it's a great way to introduce who you are and what you do to someone. If it's interesting enough, it will pique the interest of your audience and lead them to want to know more. Your elevator pitch often uses aspects and highlights of your USP to entice, but it is definitely not your actual USP.

On the other hand, your USP is your core, customer-centric defining statement that sets you apart from everyone else. It tells your audience in an exciting way what makes you better, different, unique and ultimately the logical choice in your industry.

Your USP is more than just words; it's a promise. It needs to be original, exciting, authentic, desirable and highly attractive to your niche or target market. It can't be defined only by the product or service you have to sell. It has to be something the customer wants, otherwise it's pointless.

Here is an important note: One major mistake that brands sometimes make is when they can't find a truly unique selling proposition, they make one up ... one that holds no meaning or appeal for their customer nor moves them to desire or action. It rarely works when you try to convince your market that your USP is important and valuable to them. It needs to be something *already* important and valuable and you simply tap into that and use it to your advantage.

Most of all, your USP needs to be a promise you can keep. In the marketing realm, it is akin to your brand promise. If you fail to live up to your own hype, your reputation is trashed and your brand is severely damaged or fails. One example of this is Goldman-Sachs, whose motto is *"Our client's interests always come first."* We all know that promise wasn't kept!

The challenge with USPs is as more and more brands flood each market, it becomes so much more difficult to find a USP that no one else has taken or framed in a way that makes you stand out and appear better than the rest. And when you do find one, watch out because your competitors will be right on your heels looking to copy it.

Once your competition starts using your USP, you have to evolve your current USP or find a new one because even though you're the *first*, you're not the *"only"* and that's all that matters in the branding game.

When writing your USP, don't make the mistake of trying to sell your customer what you think is important. The best way to go about it is to find out what your customers need, think is important, etc. and then use your USP to show how you encompass that better than anyone else.

There are six basic steps to building a powerful USP:

Understand your niche and know your ideal customer and the problems they face intimately.

Answer this question: "I am unique because of *(my buyer/audience)*." You've already done this in Phase one so have your data in front of you to use for this exercise.

Have a clearly defined offer for which your ideal customer will go crazy

Answer this question: "I am unique because of *(what I sell)*." This is the solution to the above problem(s). For example, if your market is made up of DIYers and house flippers and their biggest problem is how to save money on plumbing costs by doing it themselves, then your offer should address that issue and be part or all of the solution. You've already started refining this earlier in Phase Two, so have your data in front of you to use for this exercise.

Find your own unique angle, twist, spin or perspective

Answer this question: "I am unique because of *(my special angle or perspective)*." Start brainstorming now for what is unique and special about your offer that will draw in customers like bees to honey. Is it your price, location, something you do or don't do, your packaging, quality, guarantee, customization, features, benefits, etc.? What makes you YOU?

Add a 'negative promise' (something your customers will benefit from because you don't do it even though your competitors do)

Answer this question: "I am unique because of *(what I don't do)*." For example, if you're selling a DIY plumbing guide for beginners you could say "No plumbing experience required – even a child could learn to install a full bathroom suite with our step by step instruction manual!"

Put a time frame on a positive aspect

Answer this question: "I am unique because of *(my time promise)*." By adding a positive time frame, such as "even a child could install a complex bathroom suite in under six hours!" you increase desire and anticipation, as well as build up a powerful promise and expectation in the minds of your audience.

Throw in an "or else" or "if/then" clause or conditional guarantee

Answer this question: "I am unique because of *(my guarantee)*." You could say "**if** you can't install that sink on your fist try, **then** we'll refund you the full cost of DIY Plumbing Guide back. But wait that's not all! We'll even pay to have a professional come and fix it for you!" Then you have a fabulous and solid guarantee that is unique, powerful and persuasive. After all, if you're willing to pay us to hire a professional if we don't learn how to do it ourselves through your book, then you have immense faith and belief in your product or service.

USP vs. Value Proposition vs. Positioning

At this point, let me distinguish between all three of these terms.

A **Value Proposition** can be defined as a clear and definitive expression or statement of the concrete outcome, experience or direct benefit of using your products and/or services. According to Jill Konrath, "a Value Proposition is a clear statement of the tangible results a customer gets from your products or services." J. Michael Gospe Jr. highlights that value propositions "are broad in nature and are a direct output of a company's business strategy." They reflect your brand promise along with all the primary benefits offered to multiple market segments and the price the customer pays for those benefits. Value propositions refer to the "big picture." Product marketers are usually responsible for developing the value proposition." The value proposition is a strategy for your product/service and tactics. Some examples include Dropbox: "Your Stuff, Anywhere" and Match.com: "1 in 5 Relationships Start Online & More of Them Start at Match.com."

A **Unique Selling Point (USP)** is a specific aspect (or set of aspects) from your value proposition that differentiates a product or service from all other similar products or services from your competitors. The key here is that it must be truly unique and not easily copied or reproduced by your competition. Your unique aspects should somehow be singular, exclusive and one-of-a-kind to you and your brand. It's only when your product/service truly has a unique, "no-one-else-has-it" aspect that has a clearly defined reason to buy from you (instead of anyone else), regardless of price. When you find out what that is, then you have your USP. Examples are Domino's Pizza: "You get fresh, hot pizza delivered to your door in 30 minutes or less -- or it's free." Head & Shoulders: "You get rid of dandruff." Cleverly written USPs will often show up as company tagline as well. For example, M&M's: "The milk chocolate melts in your mouth, not in your hand" or FedEx: "When it absolutely, positively has to be there overnight."

A **Positioning Statement** differs from a value proposition and USP in the following way because they are a subset of a value proposition and broader than a USP. *J. Michael Gospe Jr.* emphasizes that, "positioning statements are used in marketing communications programs and activities." The positioning statement includes the target audience product name, category, benefit and competitive differentiation. Price is not a component of the positioning statement. Most importantly, positioning statements represent a plea for single-mindedness when it comes to executing specific marketing messages aimed at very specific audiences.

While the value proposition reflects the wider range of primary benefits offered, the positioning statement points a laser beam at only the most relevant benefit and points of competitive differentiation that are meaningful to the persona." Positioning statements are usually developed by product marketers with input from corporate marketers. Used properly, a positioning statement can be a guide for overall marketing strategy and tactics.

A positioning statement usually follows this format:

Positioning Statement Template

To: _____
(Target Personas)

_____ is the one
(Product Name)

_____ that
(Category)

_____ unlike
(Key Customer Benefit)

_____ .
(Nearest Competitive Alternatives)

KickStart

Copyright 2009 KickStart Alliance

Source:https://marketingcampaigndevelopment.wordpress.com/2009/12/08/do-we-really-need-a-positioning-statement/

Brand Archetype And Personality

Some of the least understood of the branding factors are the importance of archetypes and personalities in developing your brand persona.

What is the difference between the two? Think of it this way: an archetype is a personality category, while the personality is an amalgam of the attributes and behaviors that make up the archetype. The terms are often used interchangeably which creates some confusion. For example, an athlete is the archetype. Discipline, focus, hard work, etc. are the attributes of the personality of that archetype.

Brand Archetypes

Another important part of your brand is choosing the archetype and personality for your business. This creates the identity for your brand. The concept is straight forward. The owners of great brands understand the need to craft, nourish and continuously reinterpret a unique identity or meaning of their brand that resonates deeply with their customers. The better the resonation, the greater the likelihood your brand will have a raging fan base comprised of loyal advocates. Think of an archetype like a template of a persona used in fiction and non-fiction story plots. For example, the dashing rebel, the beautiful princess, the gallant knight, the carefree swashbuckler. These are templates for characters with which you are familiar and can identify.

Archetype	Motivation	Motto	Core Desire
Creator	Stability & Control	If it can be imagined, it can be created.	Create something of enduring value.
Caregiver	Stability & Control	Love your neighbor as yourself.	Protect people from harm.
Ruler	Stability & Control	Power isn't everything. It's the only thing.	Control
Jester	Belonging & enjoyment	If I can't dance I don't want to be part of your revolution.	To live in the moment with full enjoyment.
Regular Gal/Guy	Belonging & enjoyment	All mean and women are created equal.	Connection with others.
Lover	Belonging & enjoyment	I only have eyes for you.	Attain intimacy and experience sexual pleasure.
Hero	Risk & mastery	Where there's a will, there's a way.	To prove one's worth through courageous and difficult action.
Outlaw	Risk & mastery	Rules are meant to be broken.	Revenge or revolution.
Magician	Risk & mastery	It can happen!	Knowledge of the fundamental laws of how the world or universe works
Innocent	Independence & fulfillment	Free to be you and me.	To experience paradise.
Explorer	Independence & fulfillment	Don't Fence Me In.	The freedom to find out who you are through exploring the world.
Sage	Independence & fulfillment	The truth will set you free.	The discovery of truth.

Source: http://thesocializers.com/thearchetypes/

In the book, *Discover Your Storybrand* by Cindy Atlee, she talks about 12 story archetypes that make up most stories used by companies in professional branding. In addition, each of these archetypes has a theme that weaves together the core elements of your story into a predictable direction.

The chart above also shows the motivation, motto and core desire of each of the 12 archetypes.

Brand Personality

While the brand archetypes create the platform for a brand's identity, a brand's personality is what makes it real. Simply stated, it's a set of human characteristics that are attributed to a brand and company.

A brand personality is something to which the consumer can relate and governs how the brand behaves with its customers. In addition, an effective brand will increase its brand equity by having a consistent set of personality traits. This is the added-value that a brand gains, aside from its functional benefits. According to Aaker, in his research work published in the *Journal of Marketing*, there are five main dimensions of brand personality: excitement, sincerity, ruggedness, competence and sophistication. They can be broken down into further into sub-components.

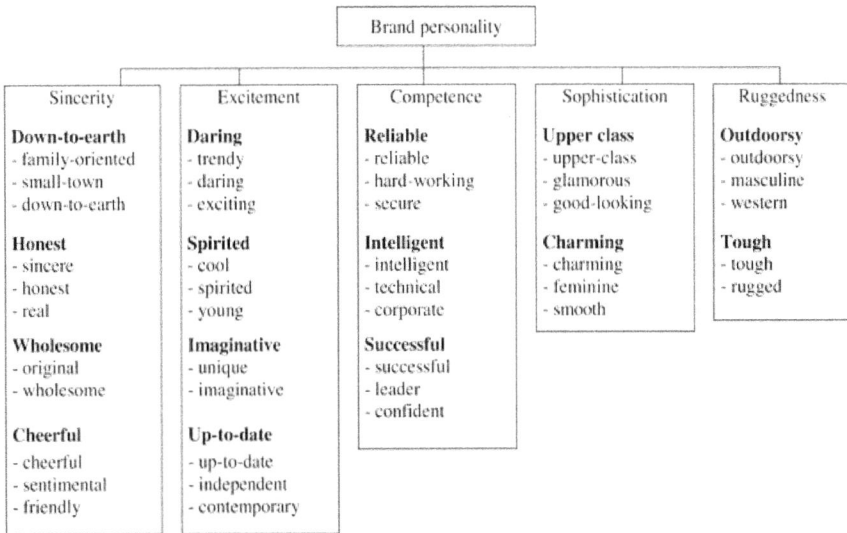

Figure 1. Brand Personality Scale.
Source: Aaker, J. (1997). Dimensions of brand personality (p. 352). *Journal of Marketing Research, 34*(3), 347-356. doi: 10.2307/3151897

Source: http://www.scielo.br/scielo.php?script=sci_arttext&pid=S1807-76922012000200004

The advantages of having a strong brand personality include the following:

1. Provides a vehicle for customers to express and relate to their own identity

2. A brand personality is a metaphor, which can suggest the kind of relationship the customer can have with the brand.

3. It can be a sustainable point of differentiation because it is more difficult to copy a personality than a product or service. If done properly, it can be both distinctive and enduring.

4. Brand personality helps to represent the features, benefits, feelings and persona of a brand. In addition, it provides the basis of a brand's image.

The chart below show which of these traits are most correlated with the Big 5 personality dimensions:

FIVE DIMENSIONS OF BRAND PERSONALITY

NAME	DIMENSION	TRAITS WITH THE HIGHEST ITEM-TO-TOTAL CORRELATION
Sincerity	1	Domestic, honest, genuine, cheerful
Excitement	2	Daring, spirited, imaginative, up-to-date
Competence	3	Reliable, responsible, dependable, efficient
Sophistication	4	Glamorous, pretentious, charming, romantic
Ruggedness	5	Tough, strong, outdoorsy, rugged

Source: http://pivotcon.com/how-the-big-five-personality-traits-impact-your-brand-community/

The Power Of Stories

If you ever read a fiction novel that you couldn't put down, you already know about the immense power that can come from storytelling.

From as far back as we can remember, even in the days of the caveman, we used visual images painted on rocks and cave walls to tell our stories and leave our mark on the world. Once language became widespread, we told our stories verbally and through hand gestures and body movements around campfires. We eventually adapted language into written words and music, so our stories could be preserved and retold for all future generations.

Today we have so many avenues for storytelling, from books and music to social media and blogs. In fact we grow up with the comfort and adventure of stories – from lullabies to fables, from parables to books and movies – our lives are made up of a series of interlinked stories and narratives that help shape our choices and who we are.

This is because stories are an integral part of our global consciousness; they are ingrained in our psyche and DNA. Our brains are actually wired to create and understand stories and we process these imagined experiences the same way we do 'real' experiences. To our brain, there's no difference between a story and 'real life'.

There are many psychological reasons behind their power and why they have become the main way to communicate over the centuries, so let's look at a few:

1. They link us back to our primal selves and ancestors through traditions, legends, myths, archetypes and symbols.

2. They reveal inner truths, universal principles and deeper meanings or morals.

3. They are timeless and they transcend language, culture and age.

4. They give us instruction, teach us, help us find meaning, discover ourselves and impart wisdom and understanding.

5. They open the door to our imagination and unlock creativity and inspiration.

6. They help us connect with others and with the storyteller. We identify with the characters and their trials and triumphs. It helps us to feel we're not alone.

7. They take us on journeys, give us experiences we might otherwise never have and help us see things from another perspective.

8. They elicit specific behavior by drawing out certain emotions from within us, such as empathy, love, compassion, rage, fear and loyalty.

9. They influence and shape our decisions, beliefs, values and identities.

10. They are easier to remember than bullets, word lists or normal sentences. Studies show that learning through stories may enhance memory retention up to seven-fold! This allows us to process large amounts of info in smaller chunks so we understand and recall their meaning more easily.

Nothing else has this level of power over us. We judge people based on their stories and we accept people into our lives because of their experiences. Some of the most successful people on the planet are great orators and story tellers (and that's often *why* they are so successful).

Stories are the undercurrent of nearly every choice we make, because behind every person lies a story of who they are, how they got there and what they stand for. We fall in love based on a story. We are drawn to certain faiths based on a story. We watch stories on TV and read stories in books.

We admire speakers who tell us personal stories and our news is one story after another.

And of course, we write our own stories, in the form of our lives, every single day.

So doesn't it make sense that we also **buy** based on stories?

Yet the one thing most brands, entrepreneurs and businesses lack is ... a compelling story. Those rare few that have one, *a powerful and persuasive one that is,* are the brands that have become global and timeless icons to us.

Smart businesses are using this cultural phenomenon of storytelling (and storyselling) to enhance and grow their brand and connect with their audience by showing them how they both share the same values, beliefs and an underlying philosophy. The story is the mechanism that accomplished this connection. This is also an important part of branding because through storytelling you are empowered with the ability to show people the role you play in impacting your customers (themselves) and the world at large.

When you show this side of your brand, your audience and potential customers will start to bond with you and emotionally engage in your story, thus developing a stronger sense of loyalty for it – and you. If they agree and identify with the story, they will want to be part of it and help further it all on their own. When that happens, the **brand becomes a culture**.

For example, here are a couple of brands that tell a rebel story:

- Harley-Davidson's story is about the rule breakers who choose to make their own paths. They are strong-willed 'rebels and outlaws' who stand up for what they believe in. They challenge the world as we know it. They are individually motivated. They represent a release of pent-up passions. They are aware of limitations in society and they set out to break the rules and challenge conventions. They feel the excitement of being just a little bit "bad." They stand out because they do not conform to the normal.

- Southwest has been passionately telling their customers that they "LUV" them. The mission of Southwest Airlines is dedication to the highest quality of customer service delivered with a sense of warmth, friendliness, individual pride and company spirit. This company spirit is at the core of Southwest's brand story—the story of people who love to play and to enjoy themselves. The people in Southwest's brand story thrive on standing out and thinking innovatively. They hate boredom and love versatile communications. They turn negatives into positives and can get away with "pushing the envelope" just a little bit.

Also, think about the stories that are evoked when rival companies and their brands, compete for the same customer. How about Coke vs. Pepsi, Avis vs. Hertz, IBM vs. Apple and Papa John's vs. Dominos?

As you can see, when it comes to branding, stories are more than just words. They are words with a clear purpose and intention. They are written to evoke emotions such as desire, craving, trust, camaraderie, brotherhood and sisterhood. They share experiences, express a message or further a cause and they make up both the good and the bad of our brand.

And, when done correctly, a powerful brand story will express the buying criteria you've already elicited through identifying your *ideal client* and *perfect offer*. In other words, you have the power to call forth a list of emotional criteria from your customer that allows them to say "YES!" to you with total confidence.

That's an incredible power to wield!

The story of what is going on with your brand and your brand persona, as well as how it interacts and correlates with your customer's story (how they benefit), is your brand story. The key part here is making sure your customers can see what's in it for them in your story or they won't be able to connect with it. They just won't care.

Without a story, you're no more than an annoying salesperson spouting off sterile statistics, meaningless features and hollow benefits.

And if you don't consciously and deliberately create your own brand story just the way you want it to be, I guarantee you someone else will. If you don't do it, you leave it to the minds of your customers or even your competitors to create your story. You won't be happy with the results.

Creating Your Brand's Unique Story

"Clothing truth in stories is a powerful way to get people to open the doors of their minds to the truth you carry." - **Annette Simmons, from the book The Story Factor: Inspiration, Influence and Persuasion through the Art of Storyselling**

Telling a story about yourself in order to get a specific outcome or action is called "personal branding," and it was first made popular by Tom Peters in an article written in 1997 called "A Brand Called You." It's now become a major buzzword in almost every industry as people search for ways to align their values, passions and goals with their business and their clients, and find a way to stand out among the crowd so they don't have to fight so hard to survive.

Storytelling comes into play in your paper, digital and online career marketing communications (resume, biography, LinkedIn profile, Google profile, etc.), as well as in business building, networking and job interviewing.

While storytelling sounds simple (and in some ways it is), it can still feel intimidating, even daunting. Where do you start? How do you write it? What does it need to say? So many questions ...

You search for the right words and you think to yourself, "I'm too boring or average to have a story that anybody would want to hear!" But that's the furthest thing from the truth. As I said before, stories are how we process, learn and think. It's how we choose and how we grow. Your story can be exciting and powerful if you follow the steps I'm about to teach you.

Now first, the bad news ... it *does* take some deep thinking and a little work to create your brand story – it doesn't just magically appear fully fleshed out. But the good news is that there are a handful of great brand story frameworks to choose from that will literally make it as easy as 'filling in the blanks'. For instance, we've all heard the phrase *'the hero's journey'*, since it's a powerful and emotional tale told by nearly every culture in a variety of ways. Also called the monomyth, it's familiar and comfortable and it mainly involves a call to adventure, an aide with supernatural powers (or previously unknown talents/ skills), myriad of trials and final victory. We see this type of story told over and over in books and movies and some of the best examples include *Harry Potter, Shrek, Lord of the Rings* and *Star Wars*.

17 Basic Plot Themes, Story Archetypes And Character Journeys Your Brand Story Can Use

Here are 17 basic story templates to think about as a basis for your own story. Which one or two resonates with you?

1. **Passionate Enthusiast** – You live, eat, sleep and breathe your passion and your passion is now your business. These brands often grow from the founder's desire to solve a problem facing a specific group of people or a certain product/industry. For instance, the designer of the Dyson vacuum saw a problem (loss of suction and nasty bags) and worked for years to find a solution to that problem. Brian Tracy is a great example of a passionate enthusiast.

2. **Inspired Inventor** – Steve Jobs is the perfect example of an inspired inventor. People didn't realize they couldn't live without the iPhone until he envisioned it, created it and then showed them how much they truly needed and wanted it.

3. **Accidental Entrepreneur (or Reluctant Hero)** – This is the perfect story theme for you if you started your career or life path in one direction but a flaw in your plan (or a flaw in the path you chose) became

apparent and you decided to stop right there and find a solution to that problem. When you saw that your solution not only worked but people loved it, you started on the new path or entrepreneurship to market your new solution. You never intended to create and sell a product but because you noticed a problem and made it your goal to find a solution, you ended up on a totally different path. Actor Mel Gibson portrays reluctant heroes in the films *Braveheart* and *The Patriot* while Bruce Willis does so in the movie *Die Hard*, in Officer John McClain of the NYPD. *An Ordinary Man* by Paul Rusesabagina is an autobiography of how a hotel manager saved countless lives at the Hotel Rwanda.

4. **Hobby Turned Business Success** – This one happens to artists, crafters and designers all around the world. You start doing what you love on the sideline just as an expression of joy and suddenly everyone wants what you do and you're immediately thrust into the joys of running your own full-time business! An example is Debbie Fields of Mrs. Fields cookies.

5. **Likeable Hero (Small-town Boy Makes It Big)** - *Sweet Home Alabama* was a great movie that exemplifies an aspect of this type of story. Usually it's the shy, quiet and nice person that steps out of their comfort zone and ventures out into the big, scary world and suddenly thrives instead of being eaten alive. Examples include the founders of Trader Joe's and IKEA.

6. **Little Guy vs. Big Guy (Overcoming the Monster)** – This is the classic underdog story ... think David and Goliath or Beowulf. The small, weak guy with strong values and beliefs beats the stronger force that is corrupt or evil. Examples could be *Back to the Future*'s Doc Brown and Marty McFly. Another good one is fraternal twin brothers Julius and Vincent in *Twins*, played by Arnold Schwarzenegger and Danny DeVito.

7. **Smart Listener** – This could be your story if your family, friends or customers came to you with a problem or idea and you listened to them – and voila! A brand new business or product was born from the demand of your audience.

8. **Heritage, Myth or Legend** – If it's in line with your brand and your message, you can always create a mythical story or make-believe legend of how you came about and what you stand for. Myths are powerful

and are deeply entrenched in our psyche and DNA, so don't hesitate to weave a mythic aspect into your story if it feels right. You can also use your own heritage and story and embellish it just a bit to make it more interesting and exciting.

9. **A Leader Gives Back** – You've finally made it big and you're a success or you've dramatically changed your own life around with something you've created and now you want to give back to the world at large in a very big way.

   Think of Bill Gates, his shifting back in the Microsoft leadership team and the William Gates Foundation he created to fund his charitable interests.

10. **A Childhood Dream** – Did your business, talent or brand start from a dream, passion or experience you had as a child? Did a loved one die from a disease that wasn't caught in time and now your only goal in life is to find a way to test for early symptoms of this disease and thus save thousands of lives? Did you always want to be a fashion designer and you would dress your dog up in your baby sister's clothes and when you got older it morphed into becoming a world-renowned doggie apparel designer?

11. **Rebirth and Renewal** – It's the classic 'caterpillar to butterfly' story. You'll never find a better example of this than the movie *It's a Wonderful Life*. It's a story of grace, second chances, hope and ultimately a rebirth into something (or someone) better. It's powerful and it resonates on so many levels with all of humanity.

12. **A Transforming Journey and Return** – When Bilbo Baggins leaves, he has one life-changing adventure after another and then comes back home, he's experienced a transforming journey and return. We see companies such as Expedia and even Heineken using this type of story to get people off their backsides and into an adventure far away, but always bringing them back to the safety and familiarity of their home in the end. Keep in mind this can be a literal or metaphorical journey.

13. **Quest** – A mission to get from point A to point B, but filled with adventure and unexpected experiences along the way. Have you been on a journey to create a new line of organic bath oils and the quest

to find the perfect ingredients has led you to multiple countries where you've met a variety of interesting characters and enjoyed some very unique experiences along the way? What quest or journey has your brand or business taken you through? A classic example of this type of story was made famous by the book, *Into Thin Air*, by Jon Krakauer about the Mt. Everest disaster in the1990s.

14. **Rags to Riches** – From tragedy and misery to success and bliss ... this is the undying Cinderella story we all love and long for. Tony Robbins and his "Unleash the Power Within" story is a perfect real-life example of this theme.

15. **Tragedy** – This type of story rarely works in branding by itself (it's negative and often too dark), but when combined with comedy, quest, rebirth or other themes, it can add a new dimension and layer to your story. Having said that, there are examples of social movements coming from tragedy. For example, Candy Lightner founded MADD when her own child was killed by a drunk driver. Or Nancy G. Brinker promised her dying sister, Susan G. Komen, she would do everything in her power to end breast cancer forever. In 1982, that promise became Susan G. Komen for the Cure® and launched the global breast cancer movement.

16. **Comedy** – This is a favorite of many brands, such as Geico and Compare The Market (meerkat) commercials. A humorous story has great viral potential, but it's not very strong as a brand story all on its own. It's best to blend it with other themes to make it more emotionally moving.

17. **Customer Journeys** – Sometimes a brand becomes a brand through a customer's experience, support or even celebrity word-of-mouth advertising. These can often be powerful stories by themselves, but are best when weaved into one of the other 16 archetypes. Think of Zappos and Facebook as examples.

Developing A Powerful Brand Name

Up to now, we have been creating quite an extensive verbal brand identity – vision, values, personalities, stories make up a great deal of the identity of your brand. I want to take up two additional critical verbal identity components, naming and tagline creation, separately in the next two steps.

A Rose By Any Other Name ...

"Calvin Cordozar Broadus" is a name that any respectable young man would be proud to have, right? Sure. Now, think of a trendy rapper with style and flair and tell me if the name fits that image ... *eh, not so much.* So it's a good thing Mr. Broadus decided to change his brand name to "Snoop Dog" after the sweet nickname 'Snoopy' his parents gave him as a child.

And "Stefani Germanotta" has a beautiful Italian surname that brings to mind elegance, class and sophistication, but if you're trying to stand out, make waves, be memorable and create a mass of loyal and rabid fans through edgy and poignant music, a much better choice would definitely be something unforgettable, like perhaps "Lady Gaga."

My point here is that in both Hollywood and in business, ***names are everything.***

For instance, would the Blackberry phone have been as popular if it were named the "EasyMail?" Probably not. And while we'll never know for sure, the name Blackberry just rolls off the tongue and sticks in your mind. It conjures up thoughts of Summer, relaxation and the sweetness of life.

It's enviable and desirable, which is everything you want in a brand of Smartphone.

But choosing the perfect name is rarely easy and you can't expect to have a light bulb moment where out of nowhere, it just falls in your lap. It often takes work, brainstorming and a journey through creative processing to find one that fully encompasses your brand's image and message.

Your brand's name should be the verbal representation of your function, attitude, mission, vision and/or competitive advantage as it sets the stage for the visual identity and often makes the first impression before anything else you say or do.

Here are some very important things to keep in mind when looking for a brand name that will stand the test of time and evoke the exact impression you desire:

Web-friendly

Since you'll want a website for it, you'll need to make sure the name – or some form of it – is available as a URL. The last thing you want is to go with a name whose URL is owned by someone else, unless they are willing to sell it and you're willing to pay thousands to get it. It also needs to be easy to type in and not get lost amongst similar brand names and urls in search results.

Short, simple and easy to remember

While going too short and cryptic, like "Synergy" or "Arotel" can leave your audience wondering what in the world you sell or do, going too long can be just as annoying. If course, there are exceptions to every rule, such as IKEA and I Can't Believe It's Not Butter, but one is foreign and one is a tagline that actually doubles as a name, so it works well for them.

Avoid a name that leaves your audience in the dark; you want it to tell a story and a one word cryptic story is not very satisfying.

Stands out and piques interest

A catchy name sticks in your head. Think Swiffer, Kraft, Flickr, Tumblr, Facebook.

Congruent with your image, message and industry

If your brand is hip, youthful and edgy, don't use a name your grandma would approve of. And if you want to target Christians with you message, use a name that is clearly connected with the Christian message so that everything stays consistent and synergistic. Keep the same energy, voice and message in your name as in your logo, tagline, colors and brand image.

Easy to pronounce and spell

Having a cutesy name that's memorable only because it's hard to say or spell can cause a lot of trouble when your audience tries to search for it online or tell others about it. Sure, Xerox got away with it, but can you imagine the hassle they went through in their first years of branding to get it to stick? Don't take that chance; go with something unique but not difficult. Some of us are lazy and we can't spell. Don't make it any harder on us when you name your brand than it already is!

Not already being used elsewhere

You don't want to get your brand confused with any other brand and you may want to be able to trademark it before it catches on and someone else does it before you! While it's common to use same names in different industries, it's still a risk you take and in this game, any additional confusion or distraction can cost you money and sanity!

Different from your competition

As tempting as it is to rip off the name of a competitor (*"introducing the new Blueberry phone!"*) don't even consider it! You don't want to get caught in a legal battle costing thousands or millions and still end up having to change your name in the end. Just find what is unique to YOU and your brand and don't be a copycat. No one likes copycats.

Evokes emotion, images or feelings

You want people to hear or see your name and immediately feel the emotions you want them to feel. For instance, before the name Blackberry was chosen, the team who worked on it wanted people to feel the opposite of what a phone makes them feel—rushed, annoyed, overwhelmed. So they thought about what made people feel relaxed, such as a summer activity. And on that list of activities was the phrase "picking strawberries." They loved the idea but "strawberry" felt a little too slow and lazy (think of the similar vowels in dawdle, drawl and stall), so someone came up with something a bit punchier and rich. Thus, the Blackberry was born! Other examples include Dove and Joy brands. So make sure your name conjures up the images and meanings you want your customers to associate with you and your brand.

Doesn't contain vulgarity

Unless your brand is edgy and plans on using a vulgar name to its advantage (such as "Wake the F*** Up" Coffee or Boudreaux's Butt Paste), avoid going with anything too controversial or you'll risk alienating a large crowd that is not comfortable looking up, saying or promoting your brand beyond an occasional gag gift. Also, keep a look out for 'iffy' acronyms. If you have a long brand name, you'll find that people tend to shorten it with abbreviations or letters and the last thing you want is your brand accidentally associated with an obscene four-letter word!

Is unique

You want it to be as unique as your USP and core story, so keep those in mind when you decide on a name.

Fits perfectly with your mascot or logo

You may already have a logo or icon image in mind and if you do, make sure your name compliments and enhances it, instead of detracting from it or overpowering it.

Has a positive meaning

Even if you never initially plan to go global with your brand, you'll want to do some research to make sure the word or color you choose isn't associated with something negative in another country, culture or language. Kraft made this mistake when they named one of their new products "Mondelez" which was derived from the French words for "world" and "delicious." Unfortunately, they later found out that word had a totally different (and very sexually graphic) meaning in Russian. Ooops! So do your research to avoid this kind of BIG branding mistake.

One other thing to keep in mind here is that if you use a common word with multiple or personalized meanings, it may not mean the same to one person as it does to another. This makes it difficult to control the impressions your brand name conjures up, so try to avoid using something with diluted or multiple meanings.

If you stick to these 12 guidelines, you'll avoid getting stuck with a brand name you'll come to regret down the road.

Creating An Awesome Tagline
(Excuse Me Mister, Your Tagline Is Showing!)

Once you have your brand identity figured out and your name secured, you'll want to set your focus on creating a compelling and memorable tagline.

What is a tagline, you ask? Sometimes it is called a slogan, motto, catch phrase, trademark line or even strapline and basically it's a shortened benefit-driven version of your USP that's 100% focused on what your brand/product/service does for your customer (what's in it for them). Through repetition in media and online, it will eventually be identified with the brand.

It embodies your brand, mission and promise all in one succinct and unforgettable statement. It's short because it's meant to communicate your most important benefit, advantage or unique selling point in just a few words. But these few words have great power when done right. The best taglines can be measured against 7 criteria - clarity, simplicity, uniqueness, could it be easily adopted by the competition, benefit-driven, clever wordplay and brand-driven.

Now before you start racking your brain and trying to come up with something short and snappy, you need to know that there are two kinds of taglines and unless you're a big multi-million dollar company, only one is the right kind for you:

1. **Cost You Money: Meaningless Fluff**

    These are the cute and snappy but utterly useless taglines that do nothing for the brand they are attached to and the only way they catch on is through massively expensive and exhaustive marketing campaigns over time.

    Examples:
    "We bring good things to life"
    "Have it your way"
    "Just Do It"
    "Eat Jimmy Dean"
    "Drive One"
    "We want you to live"
    "We're chicken"

"We're Exxon"

"We make it better"

"Choose Freedom"

"Beef. It's what's for dinner."

"Pork - the other white meat"

"The only way to fly"

"Where money lives"

"Something to smile about"

"I'm lovin' it"

"We find ways"

"The King of Beers"

"Life's Good"

2. Makes You Money: Relevant and Benefit-driven

These are the ones that make you stop and think. When you hear them, they stick in your mind and conjure up the specific images, emotions and benefits the brand wants you to experience.

Examples:

"Because so much is riding on your tires"

"When it absolutely positively has to get there overnight"

"American by birth, Rebel by choice"

"15 minutes can save you 15% or more on your car insurance"

"The customer is always and completely right"

"The most exciting two minutes in sports"

"Save Money, Live Better"

"Connecting people"

"Good to the last drop"

"For the men in charge of change"

"Pizza delivered in under 30 minutes or it's free"

"Melts in your mouth, not in your hands"

"Finger lickin' good"

Can you see the difference? One is catchy but pointless and holds no true brand value, meaning or benefit to the customer, while the other swears an oath, creates a powerful brand promise and tells you exactly what you'll get, become or experience when you buy into that brand.

When in doubt, ask yourself – if I were my customer, would I be compelled and inspired to buy this product based on the tagline alone?

If your answer isn't a resounding yes, then go back to the drawing board and keep thinking!

Remember, a good tagline is a promise you must keep.

It should be short, to the point and memorable.

It must capture your brand's essence, match your image and promise a strong benefit to your audience.

And most of all, it should emotionally connect with your audience and evoke a specific emotion or action that you want them to have or do.

Here is a list of other taglines from famous companies.

Bringing It All Together - Your Overall Brand Strategy and Promise

It's all about bringing together all of the elements you have created until now. If you have completed all of the exercises, you have created powerful building blocks for your overall brand. You have values, stories, a tagline, personality, name, vision, BHAG, etc. and it is now time to look at all of these elements together before we move on.

Using the work completed in other chapters and steps, this exercise consolidates the work you have done earlier in order to build your brand plan on a page (or two). The final step in this process is to create your brand promise.

What is a brand promise? A brand promise is the sum total of the customer experience of your products and services. To be specific, it includes such things as the offer, website experience, transactional experience, support, reputation, recommendations, USB, value proposition, etc.

The customer expectation from all of these brand elements forms the basics of the brand promise. The easiest way to think about constructing a brand promise is to use a tool called the "brand pyramid" tool.

If a brand promise is crafted carefully and delivered upon, it is the basis for brand love, affinity and loyalty, so it is crucial you get it right. I like this particular model developed by Noesis Marketing.

The brand promise is simply the three- to five-word summary that is derived from extracting the value of all of the elements of the pyramid.

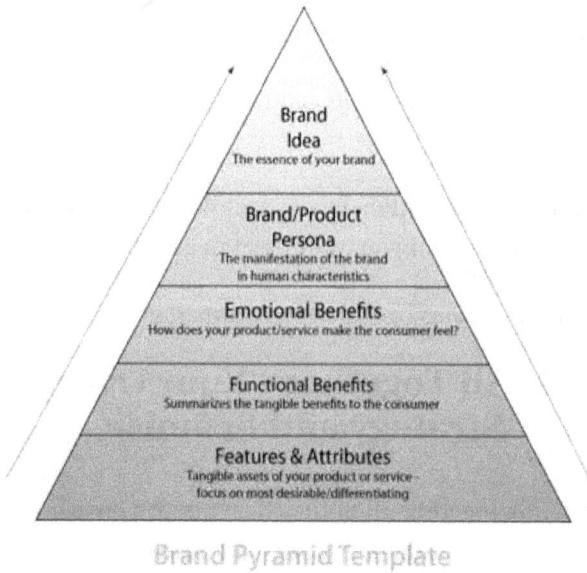

Brand Pyramid Template

Source: http://www.noesismarketing.com/building-a-brand-pyramid/

Creating a SuperS.T.A.R.™ Visual Identity For Your Brand

This next step is actually a LOT of fun, especially if you're a naturally creative person. If you're not, do not worry. By the end of this you'll be equipped with everything you need to know to either jump in or do it yourself or hire the perfect designer or team to do it for you!

In the previous sections, you have bled for your brand. You have really dug deep, found the chunks of ordinary-looking rocks and cracked them open to reveal the diamond inside. Now it's time to polish it to a sparkling shine that can be seen for miles.

Creating Your Visual Identity

What if your audience had to choose between you and 100 of your competitors, based solely on your brand's name, a few colored shapes or symbols thrown together and a short one-sentence summary of your USP? All this before they knew anything else about you or your company?

Sounds a bit far-fetched, but this is exactly what's happening every day in the business-consumer world. People are basing their choice of doing business with various companies, brands or individuals on just what they see online ... their first and last impressions of you and your competition based only on marketing materials and visual identity alone. This is even truer if many of their choices aren't familiar brands they've grown to trust.

If you had to compete solely on your visual identity, would you win out over your competition? If so, why? What is it about your marketing material, brand name, logo and tagline that would stop them in their tracks and have them whipping out their credit card right then and there, hungry to have what you're offering?

When creating your brand's captivating visual identity, this will be your task and main focus. You will need to create a compelling and synergistic identity from everything you have gleaned and refined so far in this SuperS.T.A.R.™ branding process. Everything from your target audience and brand vision, to your UPS and core story – but all boiled down into symbols, graphics, colors and fonts. (Don't worry if you do not feel you can do this step on your own. There are plenty of vendors out there that can help you like <u>Fiverr</u>, <u>Logoworks</u> and <u>99 Designs)</u>.

When used in publications, websites, presentations and other collateral, this visual identity will act as a cue to remind people of your values and brand's appeal as an attractive, differentiated product or service.

When done well, a visual identity system will enable a brand to achieve:

1. A unified look for communications, marketing collateral and messages.

2. A distinctive visual identity and graphics to consistently project your brand's personality.

3. A visual appearance that is unique and will enable you to stand out from competitors.

4. A cohesive visual identity offers an efficient and effective way for a brand to communicate with key audiences in a consistent way.

5. Provides legal protection and guidelines that help explain to customers and partners on the proper ways to use the visual identity.

The challenge is to design and define the essence of your brand through your words and symbols while keeping it congruent with your primary message and appealing to your audience. It has to speak to them and sum up who you are, what you stand for and what you can do for them.

It needs to tell a story – *your* story – and connect with your audience in a way that makes you stand out and shows you are the clear choice ... the *only* choice.

Empowering Your Brand Through Color

In this section, we're going to go over a key aspect of your brand – your colors. I can't express enough the importance of choosing the right colors, but sometimes this is much more complex and frustrating than it sounds. Some branders prefer to use their favorite colors while others look for what their customers like, even if they themselves hate it.

The secret is combining the two is to find one you and your customers are simply crazy about.

But like I said, that's easier said than done, so I'm going to spend a little time going over what different colors mean so you can make a much more educated and precise decision based on the identity and goals of your brand.

Now before I do that, I want you to read some statistics on how crucial it is to get the right color for your brand and product/service. Choice of color has some deep, psychological basis. Some of these facts are amazing!

1. 87% of consumers say that colors are the primary reason they buy a particular product. *(Secretariat of the Seoul International Color Expo 2004)*

2. When people buy, 93% look at visual appearance (compared to 6% texture and 1% sound/smell). *(Secretariat of the Seoul International Color Expo 2004)*

3. 80% of people think color increases brand recognition. *(University of Loyola, Maryland study)*

4. Research reveals that people make a subconscious judgment about an environment, company or product within 90 seconds of initial viewing. Between 62% and 90% of that assessment is based on color alone.

5. 52% of shoppers did not return to a store or website due to overall aesthetics.

6. Color can improve comprehension by 73%, reading by 40% and learning by 55-68%.

7. Ads in color are read up to 42% more often than the same ads in black and white. *(White, Jan V., Color for Impact, Strathmoor Press, April, 1997)*

8. 95% of companies use only one or two colors in their logos branding, while only 5% use more than two colors.

9. 40% of companies use text only in their logos and branding and 9% don't feature the company name at all.

10. A study of the world's top 100 brands showed that 33% use blue, 29% use red, 28% use black or grayscale and only 13% use yellow or gold.

11. Tests indicate that a black and white image may sustain interest for less than two-thirds of a second, whereas a colored image may hold the attention for two seconds or more. (A product has one-twentieth of a second to halt the customer's attention on a shelf or display.)

12. According to a 2003 Xerox study:

    • 92% Believe color presents an image of impressive quality

    • 90% Feel color can assist in attracting new customers

    • 90% Believe customers remember presentations and documents better when color is used

- 83% Believe color makes them appear more successful

- 81% Think color gives them a competitive edge

- 76% Believe that the use of color makes their business appear larger to clients

13. Here are a few key situations where color really paid off:

- A Midwestern insurance company used color to highlight key information on their invoices. As a result, they began receiving customer payments an average of 14 days earlier!

- Apple brought color into a marketplace where color had not been seen before. By introducing the colorful iMacs, Apple was the first to say, "It doesn't have to be beige." The iMacs reinvigorated a brand that had suffered $1.8 billion of losses in two years.

- Heinz EZ Squirt Blastin' Green ketchup was a major success. More than 10 million bottles were sold in the first seven months following its introduction, with Heinz factories working 24 hours a day, seven days a week to keep up with demand. The result: $23 million in sales attributable to Heinz green ketchup (the highest sales increase in the brand's history). All because of a simple (yet brave) color change. Who would have thought green ketchup would go over so well?

Here are a list of colors, the emotions they evoke and some examples of brands that use them.

Source: http://collectiveindustries.co.uk/8998/branding-colour-psychology/

While you contemplate your own color scheme, just keep in mind that color is its own language – it has its own tone and voice.

It speaks loudly to our subconscious and makes a lasting impression. Your choice of brand colors will either make or break your bond and connection with your audience, so make sure they convey the message your brand stands for and are in line with the impression you want your customers to walk away with.

5 Logo Types And Brand Signature

Once you have your name, tagline and colors chosen, it's time to merge them into something amazing ... your logo (often called brand signature in the industry).

Your logo is the key image of your brand as it's often the first thing a potential customer sees or notices about you. That's why it's critical for your logo to be a visual representation and extension of the greater meaning behind your brand. After all, you only have a few seconds to make a powerful first impression and communicate your message in an impactful and memorable way.

While we normally think of a logo as an image, such as Apple's apple or Nike's swoosh, there are actually several types of logos you can choose from. It all depends on the image you're wanting to project as well as the style, message and goal of your brand.

Let's jump right in and look at your five basic logo options:

1. Iconic or Symbolic

Sometimes called a brandmark symbol, this style is best when done in a simple yet bold way. The key here is to use imagery to convey an abstract or literal representation of your brand. The upside is that a symbol is subtle enough to leave room for interpretation by your audience. It's not as direct or finite as a wordmark. The downside? It leaves room for interpretation, so be very choosy what image or symbol you go with since certain images have a built-in meaning and it may not always be what you want or expect. It's also why some symbol logos have a variation which includes the company name below the symbol.

Examples: NBC, Shell, Apple, Nike, Mercedes-Benz, Target, Michelin, Twitter

2. Wordmark

Sometimes called a logotype or text logo, this design is clean and straightforward since there are no images or symbols involved – only uniquely styled text and fonts. The only way to stand out with this type of logo is through color and font choice, which is critical if you want to get noticed for your uniqueness and send a message to your audience about who you are and what you do. If you have a talented designer, they can help you come up with creative ways to add interest, depth, movement and emotion into your wordmark. Often times, this includes a highly specialized typeface that is proprietary to the brand (e.g., the scripted word *Coca-Cola*). In fact, the best designers often weave hidden meanings into their designs which further enforce the message and voice of the brand. When working with a designer on your logotype, be sure to try various sizes, fonts, styles and variations of thickness (or thinness) to see what suits you best. Just make sure your wordmark can be easily read in small print or black and white.

Examples: Disney, Ray-Ban, New York Times, FedEx, Nasa, Dell, Sony, Facebook, Microsoft, Yahoo!, Google, Virgin, Fender, Coca-Cola

3. Letter Mark or Letter Form

This is exactly what it sounds like – a logo that uses only letters (initials or first letter) of your brand's name to represent the whole. This is best when you have a long, complex, uninteresting or hard to pronounce name that would be difficult to portray graphically. Not a lot of imagery or shapes. Just letters presented in a fun and memorable way.

Examples: Chanel, HP, GE, BP, IBM, Louis Vuitton, D&G, Lexus, CK, Comedy Central, Gucci, CNN

4. Combination Mark

This is when just a wordmark or symbol alone won't get the job done. Therefore, the purpose of the combination mark is to create an identity that embodies a given company through the use of a symbol <u>and</u> a wordmark. This is one of the most popular logo formats out there as it offers the best of both worlds. For added flair, visual interest and a lasting impression, try mixing a wordmark and a symbol or image to create something special. You can keep your text separate from your image (such as AT&T) or you can combine them all into one element like Starbucks. Either way, if you've done your job well, your logo will be easily recognizable by each single element. Over time and with investment, if someone were to see only your symbol or your logotype by itself, they would still know it was yours. Finally, a well designed combination mark looks just as good with the elements separate as it does with them together.

Examples: Sprint, Adidas, Hawaiian Airlines, Pepsi, Taco Bell, Domino's, Starbucks, Tivo, McDonald's, Pringles, AT&T, Hooters, KFC, Quaker, Burger King

5. Emblem

This can actually be quite similar to the combination mark and in fact it's more of a subgroup of it. An emblem is when your text is self-contained inside your image, usually in a seal, shield, circle, badge, etc.

Examples: Harley-Davidson, NFL, UPS, VW, Porche, Ferrari, FBI, CIA, College and State seals

Another thing you can do with any of these options is to add your tagline beneath, above, beside or inside your design for an additional boost of recognition, uniqueness and branding. You can also have several versions of your logo in different formats, sizes and colors for difference uses. Just be sure they are all consistent and connected so the brand recognition isn't diluted.

When the symbol, text, graphics and tagline are combined as a unique and cohesive visual trifecta, it's often called the "brand signature" because it provides consistent brand recognition and a clear expression of your brand architecture and definition.

A brand signature describes what the graphic and typographical specification a brand's visual identity should be. It needs to align with your brand's:

1. Core Identity – what makes your brand unique and special at its core

2. Core Values – the beliefs, ideals, values and morals of your brand

3. Core Positioning – how you 'sell' and present your core values and identity to your customers so that they understand and connect with it and share your overall vision

4. Core Vision – where your brand is headed and what the greater purpose and mission is

5. Core Fulfillment – what void does your brand fill in your audience?

6. Core Promise (USP) – what are you promising that you can deliver on?

Essentially, a brand signature gives partners, customers, internal staff and agencies a visually appealing 'blueprint' that sums up and defines your brand, including detailed information about spacing, colors, fonts and how to use it.

8 Essential Qualities Of A Great Logo

Not all logos are created equal and while many are pretty to look at, only a handful actually accomplish what they are meant to. Make sure yours does by understanding what makes a great logo and implementing that in your design:

1. Simple – fight the urge to over-complicate. That can lead to a logo that is too heavy, distracting, unremarkable, confusing and difficult to reproduce in all mediums.

2. Versatile – consider that your logo might be in print ads, business cards, letterheads, websites, banners, videos, black and white low quality newspapers, etc. It needs to be reproducible. In addition, will it be distinctive and still look high quality and appealing in all those mediums?

3. Distinctive – doesn't look like your competitors. Be unique and stand out.

4. Targeted – your logo needs to fit your industry and appeal to your audience. You don't always have to be direct and blunt in the image or name, as long as your colors and overall style communicate what you want it to.

5. Memorable – leave a mark, an impression, on your audience. You want a logo that is so unique and powerful that it can be remembered and recognized after just one look.

6. Appropriate – make your logo match your industry, but it doesn't have be obvious. If you're a plumber, you don't necessarily need to have a toilet or plunger on your logo in order to get your message and point across. It also needs to be consistent with the brand image you wish to convey. A relationship between the company name and image you use would be helpful in establishing your brand identity. Move beyond the basic Caduceus that many doctors use on their calling card. A logo doesn't need to outright say what the company does. Restaurant logos don't need to show food, dentist logos don't need to show teeth, furniture store logos don't need to show furniture. Just because it's relevant, doesn't mean you can't do better.

7. Timeless – will your logo stand the test of time and still be relevant, interesting and effective in 1, 5 or even 50 years with modifications? Always go for longevity, not trendy. Having said that, if your business withstands the test of time, your logo will need to evolve over time as well. My recommendation is to review your visual identity system, including the logo, every three to five years.

8. Effective — it must have an impact on the intended audience and be geared towards getting a congruent and desired response emotionally or physically.

CHAPTER

3

Awareness and Marketing of Your Brand

"If you have more money than brains you should focus on outbound marketing. If you have more brains than money, you should focus on inbound marketing." – **Guy Kawasaki**

"Now we understand that the most important thing we do is market the product. We've come around to saying that Nike is a marketing-oriented company and the product is our most important marketing tool." – **Phil Knight**

Once you have a brand, you will need to build awareness and preference for it with your target audiences—existing customers, potential customers, sales channels and media. But what if you built your brand, delivered superior products and services and nobody noticed? You had no visitors to your website, no foot traffic to your retail storefront or online appointments for your professional office?

The world is littered with examples of failed brands and the mess they leave behind is not pretty. Think about Ford's Edsel car, Enron, Polaroid cameras and Atari video games. Why do brands fail? They fail for many reasons. But some of the key reasons are a lack of product/service innovation, loss of focus on who the customer is and what they want, financial meltdown, lack of relevance and increased competition with diminished articulation of what makes their brand special or unique.

Remember, people buy into your brand for two reasons—in order to avoid pain or satisfy a need (bring pleasure). They are also buying a bundle of benefits from you, like prestige, your brand's values and personality. If you can't articulate that clearly, succinctly, with enough differentiation and a strong value wedge, it is less likely your brand will be successful in the long term.

So building a brand's awareness and preference (which is marketing speak for customers who are finding, knowing and wanting to buy your brand), will require a fair amount of activity from the marketing function. But it doesn't have to be the expensive, highfalutin Madison Avenue marketing you see from companies like Geico, Coca-Cola and Samsung.

Although there are times you will need to invest in your marketing efforts, much can be done for a lot less with sweat equity. Not all marketing has to or needs to be expensive. Creating great content, PR and other marketing programs can get you a boat load of traffic, fans, shares and press to help build your brand's reputation and get your brand on the radar of consumers. An example of this type of marketing was when I attempted to trademark, "Occupy Wall Street" a few years back. I watched with amazement how the organizers of OWS and the "Occupy" movement had demonstrated day in and day out and were starting to get momentum for their cause, global attention and spawning the Occupy movement against social and economic inequality worldwide.

On a whim, I decided to see if OWS had filed for a trademark. I was thinking that I could figure out a way to hack the name to drive traffic to my own web OWS internet property and to sell previously un-trademarked OWS memorabilia. Often called "trend or news jacking," Jay Z also executed a strategy like this by filing a trademark for "Occupy All Streets," obviously a name leverage from OWS.

After reviewing all of the trademark filing information online at the US government web site, I realized that the name had not yet been claimed. Excited, I hastily filled out the paperwork and filed my trademark application to cover apparel, hats and various other trinkets and trash.

What I did not know was that an hour before me, OWS had filed for the same trademark, the very same day! A few days after the results became public record, I started receiving all sorts of requests for interviews from prestigious publications and broadcast media like CNN, Politico and of course the WSJ. They wanted to understand my angle and strategy for wanting to acquire the trademark. In a nutshell, this was free publicity for me and my brand.

I wanted to position my personal brand as tenacious, innovative and forward leaning. The media I got achieved all of that and it opened a few doors for me, although not exactly in the way I intended. The moral of this story is sometimes great marketing is about a creative idea that you can think up, believe in and execute quickly.

I believe there are core strategies that can be deployed in the marketing of your brand. These strategies can be deployed to drive your brand's awareness and preference and create real traffic to your business.

How To Create And Use Your Website As A Branding Tool

It should be no surprise that 90%+ of people check you or your company online before they decide to do business with or buy from you. In today's world, if you do not have a website, then people will not see you as a serious business. And if they find negative information, poor customer reviews and a lack of content online, do you think that would help you or hurt you in your sales efforts? I think you know the answer. Think of a website as the "central nervous system" of your online branding efforts. Everything you create, write, promote or do online will somehow be tied in or connected to one or multiple websites.

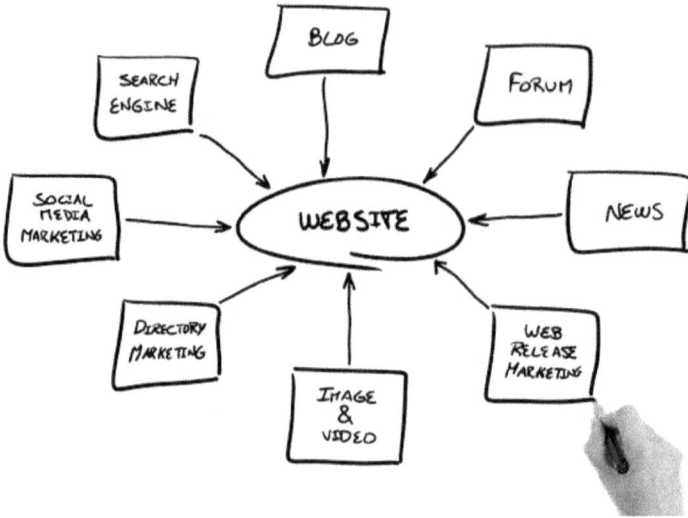

Source: http://boagworld.com/content-strategy/content-strategist/

As a brand, you have to be conscious and ever-vigilant about how you are portraying yourself throughout all your online properties, from your blog and money site to your social media and advertising.

Branding is a serious business and you should be willing to go to great lengths to find creative, unique and innovative ways to promote and share your brand with the world and connect on a deeper and more personal level with your audience.

In this day and age, your website is the main way to do that. But not just any website will do the trick. It must be a fully branded site with a particular goal, purpose and message in mind. A website is not an online resume and that is not why I am here to help you with.

A resume is a historical, backwards-looking view. Your website needs to be an expression of who you are and what you do. You want it to be a mechanism that projects your forward-leaning brand and the products and services you provide.

Some professions (like doctors, dentists and lawyers) don't get this concept and they end up building a mediocre website with poor messaging, local marketing and SEO and wonder why they are on page 10 of Google for their profession (in a particular city).

Now, as you know, this isn't a book on how to build a website, so I'm not going to go into every detail of how to build one.

If you want help and clear directions on creating a powerful and effective website, we offer some serious instruction, professional advice and multimedia guidance, go to our extended membership training program at: http://www.mybrandtosell.com.

If you already have a website set up or you're in the process of creating one now, let's go over a few things you need to have in place in order to make use of it as a successful and powerful branding tool:

- **Color Scheme & Graphics** – as we mentioned earlier, one of the best ways to reinforce your brand and its message is through color. Color evokes emotions. Whatever you chose as your logo and brand color needs to stay consistent throughout your entire website, as well as your printed material and anything else associated with your brand. If your logo is green then your website colors must be consistent with that color scheme. You can't have a green logo on a red, white and black web page. It would look terrible and that kind of mistake is bad for your brand's image. Finally, the stock or original photos you use on your site must be consistent with your brand identity and personality and they need to enhance your content, not distract from it.

- **Website Content** – the content you choose to distribute on your site should (and will) reflect on your brand. If you write in a lighthearted, conversational, casual or edgy way, your brand will take on a different persona than if you were to write in a colder more professional and dry tone. What you write **and how you write** are both aspects of your brand and are just another way to cement who you are and what you stand for. Make sure your site content reflects your brand message and gives every visitor the impression you desire.

- **Web Programming Language** – it took me many months to figure this out, but the website platform you should use for your site should be Wordpress for a variety of reasons. Trust me on this one. If you have unlimited time, money and people to maintain your website or you're building the next LinkedIn, there are other options like Joomla, Ruby on Rails, PHP and many more. Personally I like Wordpress because it balances functionality/design with the ability to maintain the website on an ongoing basis (plus it's perfect for SEO). In addition, there are tons of free or low-cost themes, plug-ins and programmers that are available to you to help build and manage your site.

- **Repetition** – keep every element and aspect of your brand consistent throughout all your site pages, social media properties and printed materials. Repetition is how connections, habits and memories are formed, so make every impression of your brand count by keeping it consistent. Research has shown that a person needs to hear or see something three to seven times before remembering it.

- **Domain Name** – when possible, use your real name, brand name, company name or USP in your domain name. That way when you put your URL on everything you do and create, it will further your brand and increase the awareness and memorability of it. Ideally, you want a domain name with .com or .net. If you are an organization, use .org. Stay away from names with more than one hyphen in it, as Google sees that as spammy. Try to avoid getting an "exact match" domain with your keywords in it (such as www.redapples.com if you sell red apples), because Google has recently started penalizing websites for this because it looks like they are trying too hard to rank high. When you purchase your .com, go ahead and buy the matching .net, etc. to keep others from getting it and confusing your customers.

- **Newsletter or Ezine** – if you don't have one of these, you should definitely look into creating one because it's a great way to spread the word and get your message out to your audience. When you design your header or layout, include your logo, website address, brand name, tagline and/or UPS and keep the style and color consistent throughout. I like Paper.li as an authoritative way to curate and deliver ongoing constant content to your customers.

- **Thank You Pages** – if you have an opt-in form (for newsletters, ebooks, info products, etc.) or checkout page on your site for a paid product or service, then you most likely have a 'thank you' page after they subscribe/purchase. Be sure to brand this area clearly and include your USP to reinforce the positive choice they made to connect with you. Keep it clean and simple, but be sure your branding and message extends to even the furthest reaches of your site.

- **Call-to-Action** – every site needs a call to action, whether it's to buy something, hire you, getting free tools and information, sign up for something, follow you on your social sites or just read your posts and interact with you. Make sure your call-to-action matches your brand and its message and that it's clearly expressed and visible on your site. Your audience needs to know where to go and what to do next, so don't be shy about showing them the way there.

- **Overall Design and Layout** – your site's layout and navigation speaks loud and clear to the type of brand you have and to its own unique personality. Is your brand loud and flashy with an edgy hip appeal? If so, then your site should reflect that. Is your brand conservative, corporate or simplistic? Then make sure your site design and color choice clearly communicates your brand's persona.

- **Social Media Friendly** — you will want all of your content—posts, pictures, video, etc. shared through social media so people can like, favorite, forward and share your content. There are many plug-ins in WordPress that can be used for this purpose.

- **Images** – every image on your site needs a purpose and a reason for being there. It must further your brand, enhance understanding, bring clarity, pull an emotion from your audience or draw attention to something you want to stand out. Remember that video and images cause a deeper level of learning and attention than written or spoken words. This concept is often called the "Cone of Learning". Also, make sure your images all convey a clear and strong branded message and that they are congruent with your brand in every way. Use them to tell stories. Finally, please note that if you're not using your own images, do not copy and paste interesting images you find on the web. This violates copyright laws and you can be sued. The right approach is to go to low cost stock photo sites like iStockPhotos, Deposit Photos or 123RF and pay to get a license to use their photos. I am sure you will find many that you'll like and often the prices aren't as high as you would think.

- **Fonts and Typefaces** – pick a single or set of fonts and sizes to use for your brand and keep them consistent throughout all your marketing and site pages. Changing your font can cause a disconnect with your audience and actually hurt your brand, especially if your logo uses a specific style or look.

- **Favicon** – adding a favicon to your website, you can help your website stand out and be recognizable when your audience bookmarks it. Most modern browsers support favicons, so definitely take advantage of them by using a smaller version of your logo or your brand initials to set yourself apart.

- **Innovation** – if you want to stand out, look for innovative and creative ways to implement things on your site that encourage interaction and sharing, such as contests, games, relevant widgets, Easter eggs (like Google does), etc. Integrate your Twitter, Facebook and other social media feeds. If you find ways to keep people on your site longer and have them coming back for more, you've got a potential goldmine on your hands.

- **Mobile Adaptive** – is a web design approach aimed at crafting sites to provide an optimal viewing experience—easy reading and navigation with a minimum of resizing, panning and scrolling—across a wide range of devices (from mobile phones to tablets and desktop computer monitors). As the world shifts to smart phones and tablets (they are selling more of them now than desktops and notebooks), so must your website. Nobody likes to browse a website meant for a large monitor on a smart phone. Mobile responsive is different and simpler to implement than mobile adaptive. Mobile responsive actually scales down an existing website to a mobile device (think tiny). Mobile adaptive actually serves up different navigation and menus for your website, depending on the device you are using to browse. It is a better, but more expensive solution. Finally, please know that Google now penalizes websites that are not optimized for mobile viewing and navigation.

In Order To Build Your Website, You Have Three Options

First, you can hire a web design company, preferably with some graphics design capability, to build you a customized website to suit your brand. This would probably cost $500-2,500 or more, depending on whether it's a simple Wordpress blog or a fully-fledged e-commerce site with hundreds or thousands of products.

Second, you can do it yourself. What you would need to do is get a domain name, find a hosting company (I use Host Gator and Kajabi) and purchase a Wordpress theme for your website. I like the themes from Theme Forest, WooThemes, Elegant Themes and RocketTheme. By the way, if you find a site(s) that you like, you can find out what theme they are using (for Wordpress) at "What WP Theme is That?"

The third way to build a website is to use an automated website builder. An automated web site builder builds a website in an intuitive, menu-driven way (no plug-ins). The service provider charges you a higher price for the site and the hosting. If you want to change your web site hosting at a future time, you need to "buy" the website from the host company. It still may be a good option for some of you. If you want to go down this path, check out Wix.com and Web.com. In addition, they have designers you can connect with to build your custom site for an additional fee.

Building A Stellar Customer Experience

Earlier in this book I wrote about how customer touch points can be part of the brand identity. Now I want to dive deeper into how you create inbound and outbound customer experiences. After all is said and done, nothing you do to brand will matter if your customer experience is lacking or not true to customers' expectations about your brand.

Did You Know?

According to Harvard Business School's James Allen, 80% of businesses state that they offer a great customer experience. This is in great contrast to the 8% of customers who feel the same way.

So while you think you're creating a positive experience for your customer, chances are, you're not.

In fact, here are a few very interesting stats about the customer experience:

- 97% of people polled said that their online experience influenced whether or not they would purchase a product or service from a brand.

- 65% have had an online experience that changed how they thought about a brand or their products/services.

- Customers are 58% more likely to tell their friends about a company that delivers relevant customer experience.

- 73% would expand their purchases if they had a superior customer experience.

- 89% of consumers have stopped doing business with a brand (and started using a competitor) after having a negative customer experience.

- 47% of customers expect answers within 24 hours when they ask a brand online for help.

- 47% say they are more likely to spend more with brands after they have positive experiences.

- 99% of brands don't ask their customers (specifically on social media) to help with product innovation.

- 93% of brands don't reward their most active contributors.

- 91% of customers never hear back from a brand after tweeting about them.

So What Exactly Is The "Customer Experience"?

To quote Wikipedia:

> *"**Customer experience (CX)** is the sum of all experiences a customer has with a supplier of goods and/or services, over the duration of their relationship with that supplier. From awareness, discovery, attraction, interaction, purchase, use, cultivation and advocacy. It can also be used to mean an individual experience over one transaction;*

*the distinction is usually clear in context. The customer experience has emerged as the single most important aspect in achieving success for companies across all industries" - **Peppers and Rogers 2005**.*

To be clear, customer service is not the same as customer experience, although service and support are a very important part of that experience. Your customer's experience with you is a culmination of how they feel about every interaction with you, from your website's look and feel, navigation and message to your product selection, checkout process and customer service. It's what they think about you, how they feel about you, what they associate with you, how you've treated them, how you've helped them and the value and overall experience you provide.

A S.T.A.R.™ brand is one that manages its customer experience in an advantageous way and takes an aggressive approach to control, shaping the experiences and interactions of their customers at every point along the way.

An example of one company that does this well is Amazon. Their customer experience is one of the best out there and every day CEO Jeff Bezos works to make it even better.

With over 88 million users, they've begun to perfect the art of customer experience through their low prices, fast delivery, reliability, consistently enforced guarantees, high standards, cutting edge innovation and the fact that you rarely have to deal with a live customer service rep to get any problems fixed.

We could stand to take a page out of their book. In fact, they sell their customer experience in such areas as web hosting, eCommerce storefronts, clouds storage, Kindle reader and payment processing. Others examples of stellar customer experience brands include Lexus, Singapore Airlines, Zappos, Virgin Air and Sweetwater Music.

Customer experience is a rather new development in marketing that has evolved over the last 10 to 20 years. The premise is that the Pareto principle (also known as the "80-20 Rule") applies to business/customers, meaning you have 20% of the customers deliver approximately 80% of the revenue and profits. As a result, because they are so important to your business' viability, they deserve a VIP approach in their interactions with you and your brand, assuming you know who they are.

The second premise is all of your customers can be classified in a particular way in terms of their strategic value to you and their stage of their relationship with you and your brand. The customer pyramid below illustrates this concept.

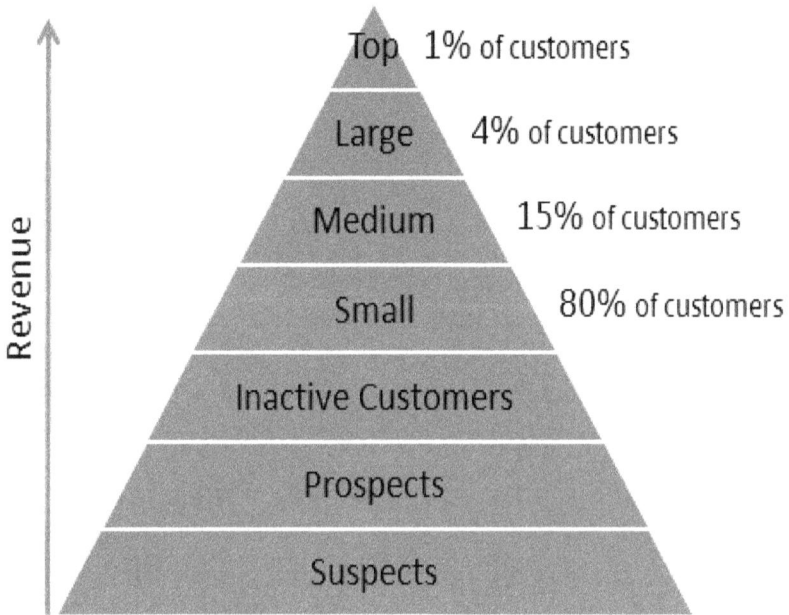

Source:http://www.expertprogrammanagement.com/2011/06/customer-marketing-and-relationship-management-currys-pyramid/

In your business, you will want to move the appropriate people up the pyramid, because the higher up they are, the more money they are worth. Airlines do this very well with their Platinum, Gold and Silver frequent flyer programs and lounges.

For example, moving people from suspects to prospects or inactive customers to active and small customers. This is not easy and takes a lot of work and dedication to accomplish.

In order to move them up the pyramid, you need to move people from prospects to customers. In addition, you need to take the 'dissatisfiers' (things people don't like) and correct them so they turn into satisfiers (things they do like) or at least have a neutral feeling about them. At the same time, you take the satisfiers and make them like these even more. In other words, the whole point is this ... find out what is important to them and how you can make (and keep) your customers happy and satisfied and always promptly fix the important areas where they are dissatisfied.

This means you need to have a strong knowledge of your customers' needs backed by thorough research, insight, experience and data that comes from your business.

Your Success Depends On Your Level Of Customer Experience

There is a direct relationship between brand loyalty and the level of customer experience you deliver. Developing a superior customer experience is critical in order to turn first time customers into lifelong customers and turning existing customers into raving, loyal fans and advocates of your brand. In addition, it helps to keep loyal customers from jumping ship and going to a competitor's products and services.

In order to do this, you need to focus your strategy on two main areas. First, you must automate your business and be confident in the predictability of your key processes. For example, is your website fast and responsive enough to handle and accommodate the growing number of tablet and smart phone users? Is your payment service secure? Does your server have 99.9% up-time and the right amount of speed? Does the staff answer the phone within 1-2 rings?

Second, create a customer experience to reflect what your customers find valuable. This means researching and identifying what your competitors are doing well (and poorly), understanding your customers' wants, conscious needs, unconscious needs and issues and delivering back to them a solution that meets their needs in a superior way.

Remember, ultimately this is not about your product or service. It's about everything that surrounds it, from awareness and consideration, to using, learning and supporting your products. If you do this well, it can be a source of real competitive differentiation and advantage. It goes without saying that the customer experience is scaled to the value your customer provides you. I call this process "ACOILUSD," which is an acronym for awareness, consideration/ choice order, install, learn, use, support and dispose. It simply means that you deliver improved customer experiences across all of the touchpoints and interactions you have with your customers during their buying journey.

SuperS.T.A.R.™ Marketing Blueprint

This section is all about how to market, advertise and spread the word about your brand to everyone in your target audience. I will teach you how to build it from the ground up by bringing relevant, targeted and hungry people to your brand's door through a variety of powerful methods.

That being said, there are tons of different marketing plan formats you could follow or create and every one of them has their virtues and great ideas. But for the sake of time and space, I'm going to show you one that I find clean, clear, short and simple. It's just enough to actually get you started and give you a direction and purpose, but not so complex that it will overwhelm or terrify you.

Because if you feel overwhelmed, it's highly unlikely you will actually take any action on it – and that's the whole point of a marketing blueprint!

So let's move on to the 6-Step S.T.A.R.™ Marketing Blueprint.

6-Step S.T.A.R.™ Marketing Blueprint

1. Where are you now and where do you want to be?

In the first chapter, we had to self-assess your current situation, your SWOT, your competitors' SWOT and your goals for the future. Take all of the info you've gathered and written down in the earlier chapters and dig deep to create an outline of where you are in comparison to where you want to be.

Answer questions such as:

- How long have I been in business?

- What assets (in all areas from money and USP to training and time) do I have?

- What do I need that I don't have and how can I get it?

- What kind of marketing am I doing? Is it working? What am I spending?

- What is my competition doing? Can I do it better, faster, cheaper, simpler, etc?

- Where do I want my brand to be in six months? In a year? In five or ten years?

- What are my short-term and long-term goals in all areas of my brand?

- What are some general marketing ideas to get me to my goal?

If you're having trouble coming up with marketing goals and ideas, reach out to an expert for help and guidance.

2. How much money and time can you spend?

This is ultimately what will determine which marketing methods and what course of action you can take. While there are many techniques you can use to generate marketing and PR, you will need to be spending some money. What can you spend each week (or each month) on your marketing? You need to set a monthly budget for both time and money (as best you can), be able to measure ROI and stick with it.

How much are you spending for brand development, monthly costs (web hosting, SEO, auto-responders), software, PR, labor, etc? I know it's challenging at first, but just jump in and you can adjust as you get a feel for everything. Plan out the first year, but also set shorter-term goals for a few months so you can check how you're doing and see if you need to change course based on your ROI and market feedback.

Unless you are somebody like "Joe the Plumber," one thing to keep in mind here is that rarely will you find any marketing efforts that will instantly create great results for you; they are cumulative over time. It may take months before you see the result you want (or even years), which is why it's absolutely crucial to have as many marketing methods (or "fishing poles in the water") as you can afford to create and manage. The more you have out there, the better the chance you have to catch multiple fish! Once you have created your brand, it's the cumulative efforts over time from a variety of focused marketing efforts that will yield the best results.

3. Where are you falling short?

Once you have a basic plan that you've begun to put into practice, it's time to step back and see how it's working. When you evaluate your marketing plan, what you're looking for are weaknesses and gaps. Where do you fall short of the mark? This may not sound overly difficult, but it's more challenging than you think and sometimes, you really need an outside source to help you see the bigger picture of how your business and brand compares to others that are similar. Picking the brains of a Mastermind group of similar successful businesses or hiring a professional marketing team can help dramatically because they aren't so closely attached to your plan and its success and can see your business more objectively.

In other words, you can often feel strongly (for better or for worse) about your marketing plan and have a difficult time letting go or changing it on your own because you're attached to it and invested in it. Letting go can be hard, but by being open to the advice of a pro or group that is already accomplishing what you want to accomplish, you can cut the ties of those methods that aren't working and learn to embrace new and more beneficial ways of growing your brand.

When evaluating your plan to find the gaps, problems or weaknesses that need improvement, there are four main areas to focus on – traffic, reach, engagement and conversion. To be even more specific, it's all about taking leads and turning them into sales.

Traffic is the currency of the internet and resolves the question, what if you build your brand and they don't come? You have a strong and clearly defined brand and a position because you have done all of the exercises in this course so far, but you check your Google Analytics, phone calls or e-book download numbers are dismally low.

Perhaps you feel dejected and depressed because you have no customers or leads. Relax ... the traffic will come in due time with the right marketing, right offer, customer-centric messages and SEO efforts. Anyway, if you started with the traffic first, where would you have sent that traffic? A web page under construction? What a waste that would be! You need to build your brand, content and your website before you get the traffic, especially if you do not currently have a web site.

Now, if you have a website and are just making changes to your brand, then my advice is a bit different. In that case you'll want to make sure that you focus your efforts on directing your traffic over to your new site.

Don't ever take your existing site/domain name offline! Build your new site offline, test it, put it online, then auto forward traffic from your existing domain name to your new domain name.

Finally, not all traffic is created equally. It's all about quality. For example, which one is better: having 1,000 people visit your site but only getting two sales/ leads or having 100 people visit your site and getting 10 sales? With traffic, it's ALWAYS quality over quantity (and the same goes for your email list!). For many reasons, quality of traffic and your ability to convert that traffic into sales is obviously better than a lot of traffic that doesn't convert (unless you're selling advertising space, then high traffic matters).

For B2B websites, the pie chart on the following page shows where leads (through traffic) come from:

Source of Leads for US Small and Medium-Sized B2B Company Websites, 2012
% of total

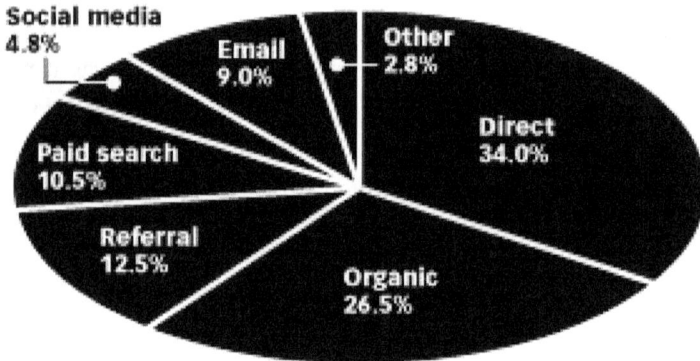

Note: read as 26.5% of leads were from visitors who navigated to the site through organic search; numbers may not add up to 100% due to rounding
Source: Optify, "2012 B2B Marketing Benchmark Report," Jan 23, 2013

150790   www.eMarketer.com

Source: http://openmarketing.com/blog/for-b2bs-smbs-the-oscar-for-best-social-medium-goes-to-twitter/

As you can see, the top three sources of traffic are direct traffic, organic traffic and referral traffic. Others sources include paid search, social media and email.

I want to define each source of traffic for you:

Direct Traffic — Direct traffic comes from people typing in your domain name or people who have your site bookmarked and access the site using the bookmark on their browser (i.e. favorites).

Organic Traffic — Organic traffic is free traffic that comes to your website as a result of unpaid search results. When you type in a Google search and you or your company comes up and somebody clicks on the result, then going to your website is called organic search traffic. How you show up is dependent on Google's search engine algorithms, your SEO strategy, web presence, content and many other factors. Google updates these algorithms constantly so you must adjust your seo marketing to these changes.

Referral Traffic — Referral traffic is used to describe visitors to your site that come from direct links on other websites, programs, promotions, articles, likes, shares, etc. rather than directly or from search engine results. For example, other sites that like what you have to say or sell may post a link recommending your site. Or people who find your link because of a guest post, a link in a website directory, blog post or through back links that may come from comments, forums and in other ways.

Paid Search — This is the opposite of organic search. In this case, you pay Google, Bing, etc. to show up on page 1 results, usually on the top, side and bottom of the page of organic search results. In contrast, PPC (Pay Per Click) is advertising which comes from sponsored banner or pop-up ads, triggered by targeted key phrases, retargeting, etc. **Social Media** — Social media traffic is traffic that is derived from posts or advertising on social media sites like Twitter, Facebook and LinkedIn. It comes because you or someone else online have followers, tweets, fans, likes, favorites, shares, comments, communications, customer conversations or profile information in your various social media sites. You can also advertise in social media in the hopes that a friend tells many other friends about your brand and products.

Email Traffic — traffic resulting from an email (with an in-house list or purchased list) with an offer, content or promotion. This traffic happens when you click on a link in an email and you are referred to a web page.

Once you have traffic, you can evaluate that traffic these ways.

Reach is the number of people exposed to your marketing efforts. They can come from your blog traffic, pay-per-click, opt-ins, affiliates and joint venture partnerships, posters and fliers, business cards, solo ads, word of mouth, billboards, commercials, website visitors, YouTube subscribers, Twitter followers or Facebook fans, as well as any other advertising or public medium. This can be a frustrating problem with any brand because you can never have more customers than you can reach, so if you only reach 50 people, you can never expect to get more than 50 customers. Even if your product or service is the best and newest thing, if nobody sees it, it's never going to go anywhere. Acquiring customer reach that is as broad as possible for your niche and is of high quality is an important part of your brand strategy.

Engagement is the connection and interaction between you and those you reach. Are people responding to your marketing? Are they actively participating, listening, discussing and taking action on what they see? The amount of engagement your customers indulge in is directly related to the quality of your marketing message and content, assuming you have targeted the right group with the right message and the frequency of the message. Once you have those metrics worked out, the best way to gauge engagement level with your audience is through actual feedback that comes from such metrics. Finally, engagement varies based on the marketing medium you are using, so keep that in mind.

For example, you can judge the engagement level of your audience on your Facebook page by counting how many likes, shares and comments there are. You can measure interaction on your website by looking at your analytics to see how many unique people visit your site, how long they stay on each page (bounce rate) and how many likes, shares and pages they visit during their stay. On your blog you can count comments while on emails you would look at the open and click rates. If your Facebook page is like a Canadian ghost town and your Twitter is quieter than a cemetery, then you've found an area that is keeping you from experiencing success in your branding and growth efforts.

Conversion is the holy grail of marketing ... getting people to do something. It is all about getting your audience to take the desired action you've put in front of them. It's the part where you 'get the sale' or get them to 'take the next step' in your marketing/sales funnel. A properly executed funnel takes leads and turns them into sales in a process that looks like this:

Classic Pipeline

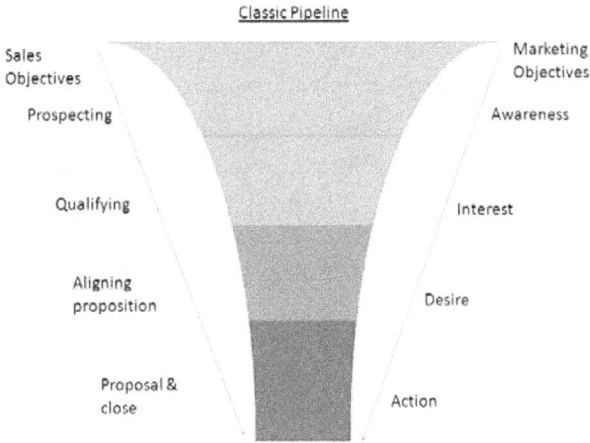

Source: http://www.toolsformoney.com/financial planning prospecting and practice management.htm

Do you want them to buy your product or service, hire you, make an appointment, call you, fill out a form, take advantage of a special offer, opt in for an ebook or video, share something with their friends or sign up to join your cause? If so, are they doing it and doing it often? As much as you would like them to? If not, then you may have a problem with conversion.

It's important to note that conversion and taking a person through a sales funnel process, is rooted in excellent sales copy (advertising, direct marketing), sales psychology, neuro-linguistic programming and consumer behavior.

To learn more, here are a few more resources for you to look at:

- *Influence: The Psychology of Persuasion* by Robert Cialdini
- *NLP: The Essential Guide to Neuro-Linguistic Programming* by Tom Hoobyar

While it's rather easy to see if any of these areas are under-performing based on your financials or sales, the challenge comes in when you try to find exactly how or why they are under-performing, where the problem lies and how to fix it. That's when you need the help of someone experienced who you trust to give advice and steer you in the right direction.

With their help, you can look at your numbers and evaluate the situation to see what can be done and make changes and improvements. For example, if you're like most new businesses, you don't have the reach that you need in order to create a viral buzz about your brand. That's a reach problem. If you have a bunch of marketing avenues in play but you're getting absolutely no response or interaction from your audience, then you probably have an engagement issue.

If you've got the interaction and the buzz going, but you can't seem to close the sale and get people to take the next step, then your problem lies in the conversion.

In every aspect of your marketing plan, it all comes down to creating metrics, measuring those metrics and testing them – driven by the content you generate, traffic and sales you deliver. What feedback are you getting?

Use these methods as a compass to point you in the right direction and find the problem areas so you can make the needed changes.

4. Fix the problem areas

Start with the ones that are easiest to fix and the ones that can bring the most return on your investment. Here are a few of the most common problems in each area and some suggestions on how to fix them:

Reach

Look for unused resources – do you have business cards with emails you haven't added to your email/customer/lead list? Add them and send them a personal email or at least your latest newsletter or freebie.

If your website is 'dead in the water' with no new visitors or engagement, consider doing a little SEO (search engine optimization). There are a few things you can do yourself in this area (such as guest blog posting and commenting, as well as on-site changes like titles, descriptions, keywords and meta data), but if your site is ranking really low (second page and lower), then you may need to hire a professional SEO team to bring out some bigger guns.

Are you visible and active on a variety of social media properties? Do you have YouTube, Twitter, LinkedIn, Facebook, Google Plus and Pinterest accounts that you post to and interact with daily? If not, set them up and start making your presence known by using them. Build your brand by providing value and support while building authority in your industry.

If you have a marketing budget, you can try out PPC (pay-per-click) advertising on Google, Facebook, LinkedIn or other search engines to get an immediate boost in traffic and exposure.

But be careful, the cost of this type of advertising can add up quickly. If you don't know how to manage and optimize your ads correctly, you could end up spending a lot of money without much in the way of positive results.

Also, you can guest blog for other complementary sites within your industry. Find very active and high quality blogs that share a common interest with you and your brand and contact the site owner personally to offer to write content for their blog. Sometimes the blog owner will ask for something in exchange, such as money or links from your site or their products/services (or you can offer this up front in your initial contact), but often times, the owner will welcome the break from writing and use your high quality content.

The key here is to show you can provide value to their audience and in doing so, you can gain access to all of their readers who already share an interest in what you do!

There are a million more ways to increase your reach and exposure, but this is a good start!

Engagement

When you feel like you're talking to a wall and that no one is listening, you need to reevaluate your message and delivery system. The best way to do this is to take a look at other successful brands in your industry and see what they are doing right. What topics are they writing about? What questions are they answering and how are they answering them? What content or statuses are they posting? What gets shared or liked? How often? What types of videos are they creating and how many people are viewing them? What freebies are they giving out? How are they creating viral buzz, excitement and interaction among their customers and fans?

Study your competition and see if there is anything you can do to improve what you're doing (there usually is).

Take a closer look at your website because you may have a juvenile, boring or outdated look that turns people off. Or perhaps your navigation is too confusing? Or perhaps your messaging is not on target? Maybe you have too much on your site and people feel overwhelmed? Does your content lack substance and value? Do you offer ways for people to interact with you through polls, contests, comments, live chat or forums? All of these things can hinder your customer's engagement and cause them to leave your site in favor of your competition.

Conversion

One of the top reasons for a lack of conversions is a poorly designed call to action (or lack of one altogether). It's common to have a "contact us" form or even a phone number on your website, but what we forget is that every action we ask our customers to take requires a great amount of effort, time and energy on their part. Why should they contact you? What amazing benefit will they get if they call you? How will their lives change if they sign up for your ebook or newsletter? What's in it for them if they purchase your product or service? It's dangerous and arrogant to assume your customers will take action just because you tell them to or offer the option to them.

Every action your customer takes costs them something, so you need to show the value in every action you ask them to take. Don't just say "contact us here" and leave it at that. Add a powerful reason or benefit such as "if you want to lose 10 pounds in 30 days and feel like a brand new sexy version of yourself, drop me a line here and I will help you achieve your goal every step of the way!" Or "leave your email here for a free 6-week online class that will help you lose 10 pounds in 30 days."

Can you see the difference a powerful and compelling call to action can make? In order for the call to action to be successful, you must find the most compelling reason why your product or service takes away their pain and meets there unmet needs.

If your product or service is complex, advanced, expensive or really unique, you may need to have some one-on-one time with your potential customers before they feel comfortable enough purchasing from you. All too often businesses send their visitors straight to a sales page or an 'add to cart' button before the visitor is ready to buy. This can be a big turnoff and may frighten some of your customers away.

Sometimes all they want is reassurance, while others just want to hear a human voice or get a few questions answered before they fork over their hard-earned cash. If you're not getting conversion, you might want to try educating your visitors a bit more through content — webinars and other tools, audio, video, free consulting call, chat and images, as well as using your call to action to direct them to call or email you for more information.

Another reason for low conversion rates is that your call to action is either difficult to find, totally unappealing or your visitors have to jump through hoops or fill out long forms in order to become a customer. Calls to action must be specific to your audience and should be focused on making 'their pain' go away or satisfying their needs. In addition, make it easy for them to sign up, join, call or buy; whatever it is you want them to do, make sure it's clearly visible and found on all pages (if possible).

These are just a few of the tactics you can do to improve or even fix some of the main gaps in your marketing plan.

Record what the stats and measurements are before you make changes and track the improvement (over time) so you'll know if what you're doing is working (or if there's still more work to do).

5. Create and Keep a Marketing Calendar

Once you have a clear idea of what needs to be done and improved, create a calendar for the next 6 to 12 months and write in what marketing methods you plan to use, what improvements to existing methods are going to be done, the budget you have set aside and any notes you need to help keep you on track. Prioritize it so that the first few months are dedicated to the ones with the biggest ROIs or the ones you can implement the fastest.

This will keep you from being overwhelmed and help keep you focused and on budget every single month. Finally, keep the calendar in a location where you can easily see it for reference and cross out the completed tasks.

6. Measure and Adjust

Your marketing plan won't be perfect right out of the gate. There will be inaccuracies and assumptions that will change over time as you gain more data and real world experience. Therefore, it will take time and testing to see what works and what doesn't and then additional time to refine and improve and then test and measure again.

It's an ongoing process and it never stops. Re-evaluation on a monthly or quarterly basis is important because as your brand and business grows and as time goes by, your priorities and the industry itself may change. Look at it like sailing a boat, where to get from point A to point B, you must constantly shift (tack) to the direction of the wind.

You can't get there in a straight line. The branding and marketing world is similar to the sailing metaphor. In order to survive, you need to change and adapt quickly and be able to track your measurements so you can cut off those dead weight activities that suck the time, energy and money out of your plan and replace them with fresh new ways that bring success.

Activate Your Marketing Through SEO
(Just The Basics)

You're probably familiar with Search Engine Optimization (SEO), but just in case you aren't, it's the method for 'helping' the search engines (like Google, Yahoo and Bing) find your site more easily and rank it higher at the top of the search results for specific targeted keywords and search terms. In other words, if you wanted to rank your dog training site high on the search engines for the phrase "how to train my dog," you would use SEO to help it get noticed and eventually rank high in Google search.

According to SEO guru Bruce Clay, "the objective of search engine optimization (SEO) is to increase a web site's traffic counts and ultimately conversions by ranking very high in the results of searches for the keywords in the search query." It's the mission of SEO to make the site's content worthy of higher search engine ranking by being more relevant and valuable than the competition's.

Search engine optimization is the science of increasing traffic to your web site by improving the internal and external factors influencing ranking in search results. It is a major part of Internet marketing and it's mostly technical in nature. It includes Web programming expertise combined with business, persuasion, sales and a love for competitive puzzle solving.

The chart on the next page, by comScore, shows the relative market share of all of the major search engines. Google is the 800 lb gorilla having market share nearly 4X more than its nearest competitor, Microsoft (Bing).

comScore Explicit Core Search Share Report* May 2013 vs. April 2013 Total U.S. – Home & Work Locations Source: comScore qSearch			
Core Search Entity	Explicit Core Search Share (%)		
	Apr-13	May-13	Point Change
Total Explicit Core Search	*100.0%*	*100.0%*	*N/A*
Google Sites	66.5%	66.7%	0.2
Microsoft Sites	17.3%	17.4%	0.1
Yahoo! Sites	12.0%	11.9%	-0.1
Ask Network	2.7%	2.7%	0.0
AOL, Inc.	1.5%	1.3%	-0.2

Source:http://www.comscore.com/Insights/Press_Releases/2013/6/ comScore_Releases_May_2013_U.S._Search_Engine_Rankings

It's crucial to optimize your website to rank at the top of the search engines because over 93% of all online experiences and transactions begin with someone typing a query (keyword or keyword phrase) into a search engine.

And research shows that as many as 95% of all users never even bother searching past the first page of results. How much is the top spot on Google actually worth?

According to data from the Chitika network, it's worth a ton – double the traffic of the #2 spot, to be precise. A majority of the traffic and clicks are done with the first five positions on Google page one search results.

So if you're not there, you're essentially invisible and invisibility does not bring in new customers. And there are only two ways to get on page one—You either pay for it (Google Ads) or you earn it through better organic SEO.

As you can see, SEO is an absolute necessity if you want to be seen, make money and build your brand online, but it's only one method of branding and getting traffic among many and it's quite complex (to say the least).

That's why there is no way I can even begin to give you the full run down on how to improve SEO your site from top to bottom in the S.T.A.R.™ Branding System.

I can't even give you a beginners' crash course ... there's just not enough time and it's such a complex and ever-changing subject that it often requires months of intense training to master.

There are tons of courses out there (such as SEOMoz, Lynda, SEOBook and Udemy) that can give you a solid foundation and teach you how to do it yourself.

For now, what I can do is give you some key things you can do to increase your rankings and improve your site's SEO.

If this is beyond your understanding and skill in the SEO arena or you outsource your SEO marketing, no fear. You can give this list to your SEO team or webmaster and they'll know exactly what to do!

Improving Your Site's SEO Results

So let's look at what you can do to improve your rankings while making your site a rich and enjoyable experience for your visitors and customers.

If you don't already have it, sign up for a Google Analytics account and get it set up on your site. It will provide a wealth of data including tracking info so you can see how you're doing and what you need to improve. Also be sure to log in to your Webmaster Tools area and watch for any warnings or errors from Google. If you get either, your rankings will drop until you fix it and resubmit the site. Google needs to validate and index your site in order for it to be graded and ranked properly. Also, don't forget to submit and validate you website on other search engines like Bing and Yahoo.

Choose your keywords carefully. Find out what your audience is searching for most often by using Google Keywords Tool. In this way, you will know on what to focus your content, home page, blog posts, categories, meta tags and key landing pages. This is also where it can get tricky, though. Don't be tempted to 'keyword-stuff' your site by putting in a bunch of keywords (or the same keyword 20 times) on the same page as Google will penalize you for that. Vary them and make sure you write for your audience – not the search engines. Make it sound natural, easy and conversational.

Create compelling content. From blog posts to ebooks, home page content to videos, your site should be packed full of rich, valuable, relevant and free content that clearly reflects the keywords for which you are aiming to rank. It must be readable, use proper grammar, be 100% original (not copied from someone else) and be at least 500 words or longer per page. Google search algorithms like longer, high quality content.

Link together to your own content and site pages. One little 'trick' of SEO is to highlight certain words, phrases or keywords within your content and hyperlink them to something else on your site or another highly ranked site like Wikipedia. If you're referring to a previous post or a video on your site, be sure to link to it. If your call to action tells them to contact you, link to your contact form. If you mention someone in the company by name, link to their bio or LinkedIn page. You get the picture. You can link to your own inner site pages several times in each post or article.

Install a set of social sharing options. You should already have all of your social media properties linked to your website through visible icons on your home page, but on each piece of content on your site, you need to have a set of the most popular sharing and like buttons as well. Usually just LinkedIn, Facebook, Twitter, Pinterest and Google Plus will be adequate, but you can add more if you desire. The whole point is to make your content so interesting and relevant that your visitors will find it easy and want to share it with all their friends. So if you have those quick little share and like buttons on each page, they can do it without any fuss.

Learn the art of 'pagination'. It's a key factor in keeping people on your site longer, having them stay engaged and it's also a key factor in ranking. The longer people stay on your site and the more pages they visit and read, the higher Google will rank you for your keywords because it thinks you must be relevant. If people stay on your site for a while, it looks to Google like they have found what they are looking for and you're providing a great source of information and education for them. One of the best ways to do this is to split up long articles into several pages and at the bottom of each page place a button/arrow that says "keep reading" or "next page." You can also use number links. For instance, if you have 5 pages of text, at the bottom of each page you can list those pages – 1, 2, 3, 4, 5 —so they can follow the links to read each page. You can also connect one blog post to another to encourage people to keep reading and getting more engaged in your site.

Vary your keywords, titles and tags. If you use the same keyword (or small set of keywords) throughout your site (such as in the urls, titles, tags, meta descriptions, H1 and H2 tags, content, link anchor text, etc.), you'll limit the terms you can be found under, as well as get a penalty from Google for over-optimizing your site. Use your main keywords but also use different variations, synonyms and related word clouds to keep things relevant but not over-optimized.

Register your XML sitemap with Google. Your site already has a sitemap, but it needs a registered XML sitemap that's been submitted to Google to help it learn exactly what your site is all about. This is important because often Google's spiders will only crawl through certain pages on your site, when what you really want is all your pages to be crawled and indexed into their search engine and then ranked. Submitting your XML sitemap to Google will help. Learn how to set up and submit your XML sitemap here: http://www.xml-sitemaps.com/

Use your keywords and phrases in your images. This is one surefire way to boost your site's rankings! Make sure ALL the images on your site, including your logo and header images, are all titled with some variation of your keyword phrase. Make each one different and use synonyms and related words (i.e., lawyer, attorney, law firm, solicitor, legal, law, lawsuit, personal injury, etc.) to add variety and avoid over-optimization penalties. Be sure to rename BOTH the actual image file's name as well as the alt-name on your site.

Check your Google Webmaster Tools for any duplicate content, broken links and images and fix them as soon as possible so you can resubmit your site and get any penalties removed. If you do not have an account, you will need to set that up.

Set up Google Authorship. You've probably seen those search results with a person's face next to it, right? Well that is part of Google's authorship program, which basically just means you can now officially connect your Google+ profile with any content you publish on your domain. Google loves this and it can give you an extra boost in your rankings, as well as further your authority in your field and spread your brand.

As mentioned earlier, make sure your website design is mobile-ready. This means that the site can be viewed in the right format and size no matter what the viewing device is. In addition, the proportion, aspect ratios, etc. for your web site, scale automatically no matter what device you have—desktop, laptop, tablet or smart phone. Mobile-friendly web sites get ranked higher, according to Google.

Although Google's SEO equations are proprietary this chart, published by Search Engine Land, provides additional guidance. Borrowing the Periodic Table of Elements format, it looks like this:

Source: http://searchengineland.com/seotable/

How to Take Your Brand To The Masses

"The masses are the decisive element; they are the rock on which the final victory of the revolution will be built." - **Rosa Luxemburg**

Having your brand defined and refined means nothing if you don't get your message out there in front of your target audience. In this digital age it sounds like a relatively easy task, but it can be costly and time-consuming, especially if you go at it the wrong way.

The traditional way to get your message out has always been to chase your audience down and push your ad down their throat until they (hopefully) give in and swallow it hook, line and sinker.

This is problematic on so many levels and one of the worst side effects of this way of marketing is that it often leaves your customers with a bad taste in their mouth and a strong sense of buyer's remorse. This is because it's often one-sided with no real education, no one-on-one interaction and definitely no bonding or connection – just pure sales pitch with a touch of self-centered hype.

We call this type of old school advertising "Outbound or Interruption Marketing" and sadly it's what's made the world go round for a long time. But in the connected, social and digital world we live in, that's no longer the case. Outbound marketing has fallen out of favor (if it ever was *in* favor) and a new, more welcomed way of advertising has thankfully taken its place.

As a brand and market leader, our goal should always be to listen to our audience, assess their needs and wants, create a desirable solution, provide value and then put this solution within their reach when they are ready for it. We should never have to beat our would-be customers over the head and drag them unwillingly by their feet to purchase our product. This is not the Paleolithic Era and we're not cavemen. Civilized marketers with their customers' best interests in mind simply do not act this way. Unless you are selling some fitness product on late night TV!

Interruption Marketing		Inbound Marketing
Responsible for <10% of clicks on the web	Search Spam	SEO & PPC — Responsible for 90%+ of clicks on the web
Higher avg cost to acquire a new customer	Paid / Rented Email Lists	Opt-In Email Lists — Lower avg cost to acquire a new customer
	TV, Radio, and Print Ads	Authoring Books/Print Media
	Billboards & Outdoor Advertising	Supporting/Sponsoring Events
	Throwaway Press Releases	Press & Public Relations
	Pop-Ups & Pop-Unders	Thought Leadership
Interrupting someone's flow of activity in order to get attention	Contextual Ads	Community Building — Earning attention organically, without interrupting anyone's path
	Outbound Sales Calls	Influencer Outreach
	Interstitial Pages	Blogging
	Trade Show Booths	Public Speaking
	Most Social Media Advertising	Earned Social Media
	Forum, Comment, & UGC Spam	Word of Mouth & Viral Marketing
Powered by budget & repetition	Banner & Display Ads	Content Creation & Marketing — Powered by creativity, talent, & effort
	Paid App Reviews	Organic App Store Visibility
	Video Ads	Video Content
Costs remain generally static with scale		Generates momentum making future efforts easier

Source: http://www.wordstream.com/blog/ws/2013/05/29/what-is-Inbound-marketing#.

That's why this new softer, more transparent and effective way of advertising, called "Inbound Marketing," is working so well. It's all about earning the interest and attention of your audience organically, rather than buying it. You could say that Inbound marketing is the same as value-added content marketing. By creating relevant and immensely valuable content that people will actively search for and putting it into their path, you can position yourself for true long term success. The chart above is a good illustration of these two worlds.

The whole point is to help your audience find you, even before they need you, by naturally being in their environment and staying in the forefront of their minds through constant and valuable interaction. When you market like this, you're creating 'brand preference' which ultimately leads to better conversions, sales and referrals.

Why Inbound Marketing Works

It's a bit sneaky in the way that it catches people unaware. What I mean by that is when people are actively searching for information or just to be entertained or educated, their "anti-marketing" shields aren't activated and you can slip right through their defenses to make a true and lasting connection with them. The only way this is possible is if your content is educational, entertaining, inspiring and valuable. If it's full of marketing promos and slick sales pitches, it's not real content.

It would be like trying to fish with a rubber boot instead of a worm – no one cares and no one wants it. But use the right bait in the right spot at the right time and you can't stop the fish from biting, even if you tried!

Through Inbound marketing, you are literally "**earning**" your way into the hearts and minds of your customers, rather than *buying* or *pushing* your way in. As you can imagine, this is so much more effective in the short and long run.

But how do you know this difference between the two? Let's break down the methods and tactics of both Inbound and Outbound Marketing so you can see the difference.

Typical "Outbound" Marketing Methods:

- Billboards
- Direct Mail
- Print advertising (newspapers, magazines, etc.)
- TV
- Radio
- Telemarketing and cold-calling
- Door-to-door sales
- PR/Press releases
- Banner ads and retargeting
- Trade shows
- Email marketing and spam
- Traditional "cold" PPC (pay-per-click)
- Sloppy, lazy or inconsistent social media (used for links instead of audience interaction)

Typical "Inbound" Marketing Methods:

- SEO (being visible on search engines) and certain forms of PPC
- "Earned" social media
- Articles
- Assessments and surveys
- Blog posts
- Demos and free trials
- Crowd sourcing customer feedback and new product ideas
- Content - ebooks, reports, how-to's and white papers
- Books
- Podcasts, internet and terrestrial radio and video (information, instruction and interviews)
- Widgets
- Workbooks
- Web pages, micro-sites and niche sites
- Blogging and guest blogging
- Videos and vlogs
- Brochures
- Email (permission based to your house list and customer database)
- One-on-one personal phone surveys
- Reference Guides, how-to manuals and cheat sheets
- Live streamed events, webcasts and webinars
- Online courses
- RSS/XML feeds
- Images and infographics
- Case studies
- Presentations and slide shares
- Resource libraries
- Content creation and value-packed articles
- Word of mouth and viral marketing
- Public speaking
- Community building and outreach
- Supporting and sponsoring events
- Press and public relations
- Networking

- Thought leadership
- Becoming an authority or leader in your field (the go-to expert)

I bet you're starting to get the idea by now, but here's another take on Inbound Marketing to help you understand it on a deeper level.

Outbound marketing is the pushy and obnoxious vacuum salesman randomly (and oh-so-inconveniently) knocking on your door while you're trying to feed your kids lunch, talk on the phone to your mother (who is in the middle of a life crisis) or changing the baby that just went to the bathroom all over himself – and the floor.

Inbound marketing is more like a conversation with your good friend where you mention in passing that your 15-year-old vacuum finally gave out and your friend casually says she just bought a brand new Dyson at half price at Target and she just LOVES it. "It's the best vacuum EVER" she says. "You should get one! You'd love it!"

Which type of marketing would you readily embrace and even *like?* Which type of marketing would encourage you to go out and get a replacement vacuum?

Inbound is the only type of marketing that allows you to get inside your audience's personal circles, watch their habits and learn the lifecycle stages your audience goes through as they interact with your brand.

This is important because different purchasing stages require different types of marketing and often require their own unique call-to-action. If your customer isn't ready to buy yet, you can lead them through an intimate process or down a specific funnel path to get them to the point of purchase, but that same path or process would not work with someone who is ready to buy right now or someone who has never even heard of you.

In this way, outbound marketing can never match up to Inbound's intimacy and personalization abilities and because of this, it's just not working as well when it comes to conversions and sales. It's still a decent option for building brand awareness and pushing products people don't line up to buy—like cars, insurance and timeshares. In addition, if I can get free outbound media in terms of interviews (TV, radio, newspapers) and press release coverage that sends traffic to my brand or business, I will take that any day of the week (for free). However, when your goal is to acquire real customers in the shortest and cheapest way possible, Outbound marketing is probably more effective.

How To Create Effective and Engaging Content

"Traditional marketing talks at people. Content marketing talks with them."
- Doug Kessler

The one main component of an effective and successful Inbound marketing strategy is content and the ability to create quality content served in the right format at the right time and in the right place. It's at the core of everything you do — from SEO to social interaction and engaging with your audience online — so when it comes to content creation, a little time and effort is required to get it just right. Using a food metaphor — if you really want a Big Mac burger at 12:00 pm, then having Chicken McNuggets at 2:00 pm would not be as satisfying to you. Why? Because your heart will be centered on getting that burger at that time!

The following chart shows the hierarchy of content through what is called a The Content Marketing Pyramid. It shows how content can fall on a continuum of low effort and frequent content and high effort and more rare content. In your branding plan, you will need to make these kinds of tiered content decisions.

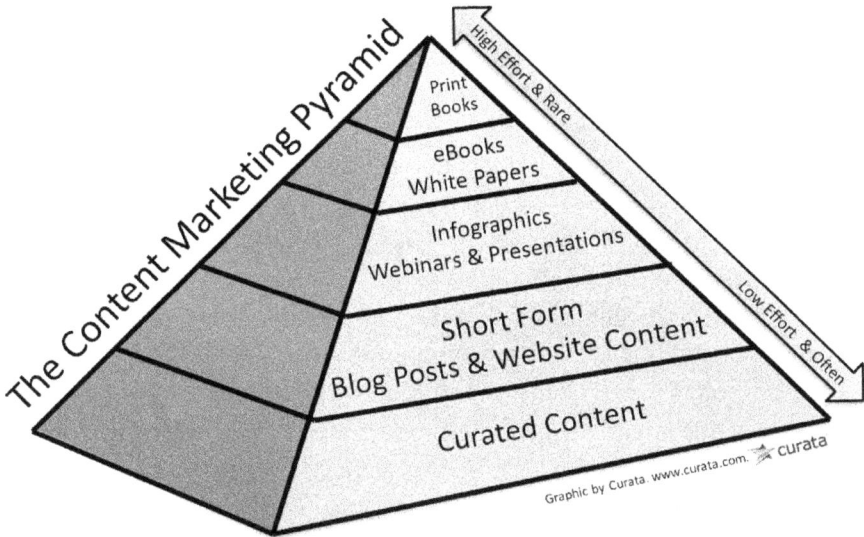

The Content Marketing Pyramid

- High Effort & Rare
- Print Books
- eBooks / White Papers
- Infographics / Webinars & Presentations
- Short Form / Blog Posts & Website Content
- Curated Content
- Low Effort & Often

Graphic by Curata. www.curata.com. curata

Source: http://www.pamorama.net/2013/07/13/5-content-curation-infographics/

I suppose almost anything online can technically be considered content; it isn't limited to just articles and blog posts. Studies have shown the most effective types of content are web pages, customer reviews, webinars and webcasts, case studies, e-newsletters, microsites, whitepapers, blogs, articles and ebooks. Slightly less effective but still great to have are online videos, press releases, social media properties, mobile content, digital magazines, podcasts and images (including infographics). Which ones you choose really just depends on your audience, your budget and the level of effort and creativity you can put in.

The good news is that you don't have to come up with something original for each one of these options. Instead, you should focus on creating a handful of extremely high-quality, value-packed content pieces and then re-purpose them into different forms or formats.

For example, if you have a great press release, you can rewrite it in a friendlier and more casual tone and post it on your blog or website. If you have a top-notch article written, take it and turn it into a video and audio (or podcast). If you have a list of steps or facts, turn them into a beautiful infographic or impressive mind map. If you have an old PowerPoint presentation, you can update and re-purpose it by turning it into a video, audio, series of blog posts or even an ebook. If you have a series of videos that share a similar topic, turn those into a product to either give away as a lead generator or even sell.

If you have an ebook no one is reading, break it down into a series of multiple videos or blog posts – or make it into a PowerPoint presentation to put on sites like SlideShare. You can also turn a series of blog posts into an ebook or special report. There really is no limit to what you can do if you are creative enough!

The main thing to remember here is that if you post written content, you have to be careful of creating duplicate content online. This can get you a penalty with Google if your site and a bunch of other sites and social properties all share the same piece of content – especially if your site wasn't the first source of the original piece.

So when you are re-purposing your content, always rewrite it to where you keep the same ideas but it's not exactly like the original. Try to make each piece of content as unique as possible.

Oh, before we move on there's an important point I need to make here. Some marketers believe that you "tease" customers by giving out crumbs of great content and give the really good content to the customer once he/she is paying client. I have a different approach.

I believe your best content should be shared (for free) with your potential customers. Why?

Because if your free content is so compelling and valuable, do you think it would be easier or harder to get people to pay for your products and services?

Second and this is a powerful marketing strategy, your content should focus on teaching your customer the "what" and "whys" of the content you're creating. If a customer can digest this information and implement a solution to the problem themselves, that's great. Those are not the customers you are seeking.

You gain your real customers by showing them the "what" of the content you are sharing. Your customers will say "great content and information but I don't know how to execute." This is your potential customer because you can do the "how."

Here's an example: Let's say you like fly fishing. You get great content on what equipment to buy, where to fish, tips to successful fishing, etc. However, if you want to know the secret spots, the unorthodox jiggers and the alternative techniques to cast you're going to need to take lessons from a local fishing specialist.

So even when you're giving awesome info away for free, there's still plenty of reasons why your readers will want to become customers and buy something (as long as you lead them down the right sales funnel and conversion path of course!).

What Are The Benefits of Having Great Content?

Just in case you aren't sure how the effort, time and money of great content creation and distribution can benefit you, here are a few more awesome reasons why content should be at the top of your to-do list for branding and inbound marketing:

- It's a soft sell approach (sharing information vs. hard selling).
- It improves your SEO ranking by increasing your links and when on your website, shows what topic your website is about and adds to your site's overall quality score.
- It increases your brand loyalty and builds a relationship with your audience.
- It positions you as an authority, expert, guru and knowledgeable leader in your field.
- It creates sales opportunities.
- It sets your brand apart from others and builds your online persona as an expert and authority in your area of expertise.
- It encourages customer and visitor engagement and sharing.
- It gives you credibility as a business owner.
- It allows you to address your customer's problems and offer solutions.

The table on the next page shows the 5C's of content marketing from a social media engagement perspective.

Social media engagement –
5 Cs to use content to your advantage

CREATION	Create original content and complement it with adequate content marketing.
CONSUMPTION	Go beyond monitoring and derive actionable intelligence out of content.
CURATION	Bring the best content in your space to your audience consistently.
COLLABORATION	Work with your community to inspire or instigate appropriate content.
CONVERSATION	Enter appropriate conversations to build engagement and trust through content.

Source: http://itwofs.com/beastoftraal/2011/02/04/social-media-engagement-5-cs-to-use-content-to-your-advantage/

As you can see, it's a powerful way to attract attention and bring leads into your marketing funnel. But only if it's the *right* kind of content! Crappy, useless and rehashed content does nothing for you, your client or your brand and can actually do more harm than good. So let's go over what makes content "good."

It's Free

There are things you charge for and there are things you need to give away for free.

Just make sure your free content is just as valuable, useful and desirable as your paid content. You want your customer to say *"Wow! If the free content is THIS good, imagine how great the paid stuff will be!"*

It's Unique

There's a ton of rehashed, word spun trash out there. You don't want to add to it, you want to create something that fills a need or covers a perspective or angle that no one else is addressing. One way to do this is to Google a question about your industry or product/service and see what search results pull up. If nothing answers your question completely, then you have found a potential 'content' hole that you can fill. Chances are if you're looking for it, others are too.

It's Valuable

Don't ramble. Don't stuff your content with fluff or filler. Every single piece of content you create needs to leave the audience knowing more or at least better off than they were before they read it.

It Exposes a Problem or Asks a Question

One way to solidify your place of authority and leadership is to make your audience aware of a problem in the industry. Show them what is wrong and agitate the issue to where it becomes a source of pain or frustration. You can also ask a thought-provoking question that leaves them in need of an answer for closure.

It Solves a Problem or Answers a Question

This is part two – once you've aggravated a problem to a boiling point, then offer a solution, preferably a solution that YOU can give them through your product or service. If it's a question you asked, this type of content gives them the answer and again, it's always tying back to you and your brand as the "ender of their pain and suffering."

It's Interesting

We have all been victim of a boring speech, lecture or book. We've all read articles or watched videos so dull and mind-numbing that we zoned out or just clicked away. Don't let your content be that. You want excitement, desire, passion, bonding and even entertainment in your content. You want people to want to read it, like it, connect with it and share it.

It Transforms Your Lead into a Customer

It must have a purpose. Your content needs a point and that point should always be to lead them closer to the point of sale and build a stronger brand. You never want to hard sell your content unless the content is specifically meant to be a sales letter or video. Decide what the purpose of each piece of content is and then keep it focused. Is the content's purpose to get them back to your site, read another article, opt-in to an email list, buy something, call you, leave a comment, educate them, entertain them, etc.? Ultimately, all of your content needs to stimulate a response – one that leads to a desired action such as a lead or sale. You want your content to take your audience on this path.

Suspect-->Prospect-->Customer-->Repeat Buyer-->Advocate

And it doesn't have to do this all in one content piece, although it can. You can literally craft content for each stage of the engagement and buying cycle and place it in the right spot to intercept your audience wherever they are.

It's Properly Structured

Especially in writing, things need to have structure – a beginning, middle and end. Start the content off with an intriguing headline, tease a little more with a sub headline and then start the first paragraph off with what the content piece is about. Use your keyword in the headline and first paragraph if you're putting this on your website in text form or submitting it as a link-building article. Give a lot of value and 'meat' in the content piece and use bullets, numbers or lists when possible. End with a summary of what's been said and a call to take another action (opt in, click here, read more, call, visit, leave a comment, etc.).

It's Optimized

This is especially important if your content is text and will be distributed on your site, blog or as an online article. Know what keywords your audience is searching for in relation to your content topic and be sure to sprinkle those keywords, key phrases and related words throughout your content. Don't overdo it; it must seem natural and flow like a conversation.

It's Readable

Keep it jargon-free. Don't use "marketing speak" that only insiders, branders or marketers know or if you must, then be sure to explain it in a simple way. Also, always try to keep it at a 6th to 8th grade reading comprehension level. If it's too complex, you'll lose them because they will spend too much time trying to decipher unfamiliar words and people don't like feeling intimidated or ignorant. You're not trying to show off your linguistics skills, you're trying to connect on their level and get your point across in a way that is helpful and easily understood.

It Tells a Story

We've already talked about the power of storytelling; use that knowledge when crafting your content and it will always be more appealing than a dry-fact article that looks like it came from an encyclopedia or textbook. Make it personal. Make it human. Give your audience something to connect to you and aim to elicit a specific emotion from them. Make them care!

It Connects With Your Industry

Always create your content with your audience and ideal customer in mind. What words do they use in day-to-day life? What is the industry or product lingo they use that makes them part of the "tribe?" What appeals to them? Do they have a short attention span? Do they prefer graphics, text or video?

Are they conservative or flamboyant? Find out their needs and craft your content in that fashion.

These guidelines apply to all content – it doesn't matter if it's a brochure, video, blog post or feature article. Make sure your content meets these requirements in order to get the desired response and interest you're intending.

Avoid Duplicate Content

One final note before we move on ...

As mentioned in the SEO section, Google will 'ding' (penalize) your website if you have too much duplicate content in your blog posts, reports, etc. Fortunately you can test your content for duplication by using services like Copyscape. What is it? It is an online plagiarism detection service that checks whether similar text content appears elsewhere on the web. For a modest fee, you can run your content through their service to identify potential content duplication (which Google hates).

Creating Powerful Branded Content That Sells For You (Without Actually Selling!)

In previous chapters and steps, I've touched on the various types of content you can create as well as storytelling, but I wanted to spend more time to go into more detail on this subject because it's truly the key to attracting potential customers and building a well-known trusted brand.

There are entire courses on content creation so I am only able to touch on the most important points to get you going and give you some ideas to start with.

If I were to give you one single piece of advice that would literally change the way you view content creation for your brand, it would be this:

"Don't write content from the wrong perspective."

Your goal is not simply to get visitors to your site or be a creative writer. Your focus should be to create the type of meaningful and relevant content that YOU would want to read and discover if YOU were looking for information about your company, product or service."

In other words, don't write your content for the search engines, don't write it purely for a creative writing exercise and don't write it just to get traffic.

Write it to answer the pressing questions, solve the burning problems and pique the interest of the people you are trying to reach. Everything else is secondary.

Before you start a single piece of content, always stop and ask yourself if the topic is what you would look for if you were your customer. If not, scrap it and come up with something more appropriate and valuable.

That being said, there is a time and place for regular old traffic-oriented or SEO-focused content and you will be creating that along the way as well, but the majority of your core content in any form will need to be the kind that answers a question, solves a problem, provides empathy or encouragement, gives instruction or teaches or even inspires and motivates.

That's a pretty special kind of focus that gives good results for your potential customers. You know when you've come across that kind of content in your own research – you get excited because it was literally 'just what you were looking for' and you felt that momentary elation, satisfaction and victory that you discovered the content, got the answer you needed, right when you needed it.

You were forever endeared to the person or brand that produced that content ... you formed an instant bond, connection and respect. So keep that in mind when you create your own content because that's the same feeling you're going for in your customers and audience.

After all, the last thing you want your customers to say when reading or discovering your content is "so what?!"

You <u>don't</u> want them thinking to themselves *"why is this important to me?"*

Your sole job is to grab them immediately – right from the headline – and show them that this piece of content is important to them because it fills a need or solves a problem in their lives and they won't be able to find this fulfillment anywhere else but right here.

Different Types Of Content

Pretty much anything can become content when used correctly, but here are some of the main types of content you can create:

- Video
- Articles (for ezines, email, magazines, etc.)
- Blog posts
- Images, animated GIFs, memes
- Social media posts and conversations
- Guest blog posts (creating content as a guest on complimentary blogs)
- Web content
- Podcasts and audio
- Webinars
- Advertising materials (online, print, broadcast, etc.)
- Marketing collateral (data sheets, brochures, flyers, invitations, cards, etc.)
- Tutorials and how-to's
- Demos
- Mobile apps
- Software
- In-person events and seminars
- eNewsletters
- eBooks, reports and whitepapers
- Presentations and slides
- Infographics
- Checklists, cheat sheets, quick-start guides
- Cartoons and animation

This list is self-explanatory, but the problem that seems to get most content creators stuck is the lack of continuous ideas for fresh new content.

Now, there are actually two different aspects to this one problem ... one is a lack of ideas of what to write about and the other is a lack of source inspiration, so let's cover both.

If you're stuck on what to write about, here's a list of 21 different types of content all humanity loves to read about – content that:

- Takes us on a journey
- Tells a story
- Reminds us that life is short
- Shows us dreams really do come true
- Is full of unexpected twists and turns
- Reminds us of the overlooked or forgotten basics in life
- Inspires us and gives us faith
- Reminds us we matter
- Compels us to take action
- Reveals secrets
- Encourages us to never give up
- Makes us cry tears of joy or sadness (makes us feel something)
- Has us laughing and smiling
- Reminds us there is more to life
- Confirms assumptions we already know or believe
- Proves good wins out over evil
- Surprises us
- Educates us
- Entertains us
- Challenges our assumptions and what we think we know
- Gives us a fresh new perspective

If this reminds you a little of an earlier Phase, it's because it's important to make sure you know that often the best content (though not all, of course) is story-based.

It's this kind of content that we never seem to tire of; we can never get enough of it and we certainly can't forget about it when we come across it.

It reminds me of the old adage, "facts tell and stories sell." In addition, I believe content + storytelling = memorable content!

For resources to learn more about the most popular content and how content is used in B2B and B2C companies, check out the Content Marketing Institute website.

vintage social networking

Source: http://wronghands1.wordpress.com/

Content is the foundation of both SEO and social media and since these are the two biggest forms of inbound marketing, I want to touch on a few things before we end Phase three and move on the last Phase in the S.T.A.R. ™ Branding Process.

We've already touched on SEO in a previous section, so let's talk now about social media.

The primary idea behind social media is to find new customers, have conversations with your customers, turn unengaged customers into engaged customers and brand believers into engaged raging advocates and lifelong loyal fans.

Now when I use the term 'social media', I'm referring to all the social platforms and communities online from the big guys to the obscure guys and all the blogs and forums in between ... especially Facebook, Pinterest, Google Plus, Twitter, LinkedIn, YouTube, Instagram, Digg, Mashable, StumbleUpon, Reddit, Wordpress, Blogger, Tumblr, Foursquare, eHow, Squidoo and Flickr (just to name a few). Here is the overall landscape.

Source: http://conversationprism.com/

You can get a larger, printable version of Brian Solis' Conversation Prism graphic online. I have one taped to my office wall to remind me of how many social media sites, options, uses and functions are out there. The Conversation Prism looks at the universe of social media and classifies each one based on its function.

There are 26 functional groupings and they include such categories as photos, social streams, service networks, music, review and ratings and many more. Another great chart, by Luma Partners, shows all of the social media platforms and how they fit together; it can be found at their website.

The power and allure of social media is that it allows you to get to know your potential customers and current customers in a more personal way. It encourages transparency, authenticity, interaction, feedback, loyalty and communication in a way that was never possible before – all in real time. Finally, social media contributes a large chunk of the traffic and visitors to your website in the form of earned and owned media.

As you can tell, social media domination is critical for your brand's success.

So that's why I will go over a broad overview of social media strategy in the next section so you can finish Chapter 3 with a general game plan to get the ball rolling! The topic of social media starts with an overview of all the various types of social media that are out there. New ones come online every day it seems, while others fade away.

Jump-Start Your Social Media Campaign By Doing <u>THIS</u> ...

Let's jump right into your social media strategy so you can start building your online presence and accomplishing your goals through one-on-one customer engagement.

First, why is social media so important? Why do we care about this as part of our strategy? When we look at online marketing, I believe there are three broad categories into which nearly all social media related goals can fall.

They are usually aimed at one of the following:

1. **Building/Strengthening the Brand** – finding your customers or potential customers and engaging them in ways that builds brand awareness and preference for your brand and your value proposition.

2. **Driving Conversations** – increasing the conversations about your brand through content curation, lead generation, engagement and enlisting customers and fans to do something. By engaging in these conversations, you increase the likelihood that your content, tweets and contests will be shared, liked and promoted by your customers among their social networks.

3. **Increasing/Monitoring the Presence** – while social media provides a platform to broaden the presence of brands that use it, the bigger benefit is the ability to find out what people are saying about you and your brand. Because of social media and platforms like LinkedIn, Facebook and Twitter, these conversations can be counted, sorted and responded to. You can track sentiments, number tweets or likes, track sharing, identify what news is trending, measure sentiment (good or

bad conversations) and much more. And tweeting has become the fastest way to share or "respond" to negative news and crises that occur within a company such as defective products, negative information, destructive viral videos (think Dominos Pizza), etc.

The core process of social media is a cycle that follows a predictable path:

listen> define> measure> prioritize> develop> contact> engage> learn

In order to get the most out of social media I propose that there are 17 actions/ tactics that need to be executed in order to maximize the results of social media. They are:

Identify Your Target Market – what are their demographics? Who is your ideal customer? What age group, income bracket, occupation, sex and location? Where do they spend their time online? Knowing this will help you choose the right social network and help you focus your content in a way that is appealing to them.

Know Their Interests and Tap Into Their Passions – what is it that drives your audience? What makes them want to share, retweet, like, comment or pin something? What engages them? You need to know this so you know what type of content will suit them best and get the most response and interaction. Find out what their passions are and encourage them to express those passions, thoughts and ideas on your platform. Focus on the unique personality of your fans and build your page to cater to them.

Decide on a Purpose — what's your reason for being on social media? Is it to bring in more traffic, offer customer support, create a following, educate your audience, generate interaction, build a community, get feedback and data, further a cause or make money? Pick one or two goals and keep them in mind because all of your content will need to be geared towards these goals.

Choose Your Social Network(s) — one recent study on social media usage revealed that the average user has two social media accounts. Some businesses and brands can manage to stay on top of multiple platforms and use each one for a different purpose or aspect, while others can barely manage one on a full time basis. It all depends on where your audience hangs out, what gets the most response and what you can handle.

Build a Compelling Page and Profile – once you choose your platform, you need to create your profile and build on it. Jump in and start fleshing it out. Add custom graphics, headers and images, fill out all the profile details and start adding friends, family, contacts, partners, vendors, affiliates, employees, current and past customers and anyone else that you think will benefit from being a part of your new social community.

Post Regularly and Stay Connected – studies show that most big brands (about 60%) post a minimum of once a day. You can even post more or start with one or two a week and build up from there.

The most important thing is that your content is valuable, relevant and that you stay consistent. You don't want to start off strong and then a few months in start 'forgetting' to post or drop your interaction dramatically. You'll lose respect, trust and customers this way. It all comes down to knowing your audience, though. If you start to see a lot of 'unlikes' or followers leaving, then you may be posting too much (or posting crappy, irrelevant content). On the other hand, you can post as many as four times a day on Facebook and Google Plus and as many as 10 times a day on Twitter – as long as you have something useful to say.

Plan Your Content — Studies show it takes a midsize company about 32 hours a month to capably handle a single social media platform. If you plan on using more than one on a consistent basis (and you really shouldn't even start one if you're not going to use it religiously), then you need to set up a system. Who will be handling updates and posting content? Who will be replying to comments and engaging customers? Who will be handling support? How often will you update/post/tweet? What type of content will you be sharing? Who will create that content? Will you be outsourcing it or doing it yourself? All of these things need to be considered and mapped out in detail in advance – before you even get started! You can use a content calendar to schedule what gets posted, to whom and when.

Create Killer Content That Gets Shared – this goes back to the previous content creation section. Be sure to include a mix of images, memes, videos, free and valuable content, ebooks, articles, lists, testimonials, how-to's and anything else your audience finds interesting and valuable.

Tell Your Users What You Want From Them – when you post something, make it clear what you want your audience to do. Do you want them to Share, Retweet or Like it? Comment or take another specific action? If you outright tell them what you want them to do, you'll usually get a higher response rate from them.

Treat Your Fans Like VIPs – Lady Gaga does this with her 'Little Monsters'! The rock band Kiss does it with their 'Kiss Army'. There are many other examples, but you get my point. Build a tribe or exclusive community where your followers, fans and customers get access to the latest, greatest and newest information, discounts and special offers, rewards or contests.

Use Your Brand Assets – be sure to connect your website and money site to your social media properties and whenever you create a new blog post, set it to automatically share on your Twitter, Google Plus, LinkedIn or Facebook. In addition, have your tweets and Facebook likes show up on your website. It's a great source of content and it helps get your work maximum exposure.

Maximize Engagement – ask open-ended and closed-ended questions to engage your readers and get more response. Open-ended questions are those thought-provoking ones where your reader replies with a mini novella, while closed-ended questions are those that can be answered with a simple yes or no (such as "would you be caught dead wearing this??!"). You can also set up polls and surveys, run contests or give rewards for check-ins, retweets or shares. Be creative!

Maintain Consistent Brand Identity – all of your social platforms should be connected with each other and share a common visual look and design (colors, graphics, font, logo, tone, message, etc.). This will help your brand so it can be easily recognized across a variety of social media platforms as well as cement itself in the hearts and minds of your audience.

Be Authentic and Human – post photos of yourself and your team, of customers and even of your pets or mascots. When you redecorate your office, post some photos. If you buy a piece of art, post photos. If you go on vacation – post tasteful photos! Social media is all about getting to know people on a more personal level so let your personal and human side show. Remember, people buy from PEOPLE not businesses or corporate entities!

Increase Your Fan Base – use contests, pay-per-click, sponsored stories, LinkedIn or Facebook advertising, viral videos, native ads, images, free content, landing pages and other methods to increase your reach and continuously grow your audience. Another way to do this is to send an email to your customer list telling them you're now on Facebook (or whatever platform you chose) and to come and join you there for some great fun and special offers. Also put social icons, badges or widgets in your site/blog to invite and encourage new fans and followers.

Listen to Your Audience – you couldn't ask for a better feedback system than social media. Listen to what your audience is saying – are they recommending something? Asking for specific content or products/services? Expressing new needs or problems? Use their feedback to improve your own customer service and products and you'll build lasting loyalty and trust.

Measure Your Success and Adjust Your Strategy – track your metrics and engagement through 'Google Analytics', 'Data Hub Activity' and 'Trackbacks' reports and social media metric sites like Hoot Suite, Google Analytics and Twitter Analytics. Use hashtags to track your mentions and to see if you're trending. In addition, implement ways to measure your conversions and track your traffic. If something is working, hit it even harder. See if you can improve your approach, use a new campaign or try your hand on a different social platform to gauge if your audience is more active and responsive there.

One final thing to mention about your social media content is called the 30-60-10 golden ratio. It helps you establish how much content you should curate, create and how often your content should be focused on selling. As a guideline, it looks like this:

- 30 percent of what you share should be content you create
- 60 percent of what you share should be content you curate (e.g., share)
- 10 percent of what you share should be sales-oriented with a Call to Action

CHAPTER

4

Reputation and Total Management of Your Brand

"It's very important for a brand to have an identity through the years, but it's very important as well to evolve because times change so fast." - **Donatella Versace**

"A brand is a living entity - and it is enriched or undermined cumulatively over time, the product of a thousand small gestures" - **Michael Eisner, CEO Disney**

Once you have established and are marketing your brand, you have to plan and constantly check to make sure your business and marketing plans will get you to your desired goals. Brands change and respond to competition, bad news and other situations. Therefore, you not only have to look ahead, but also where your feet are planted now.

One other thing I should mention is that as a functional business leader, spending either too much time on strategy or execution risks you being labeled as too strategic (can't execute) or not strategic enough (too tactical). A Zen-like balance and harmony on this continuum is crucial. It is reminiscent of a classic story about a student and his wise Zen Master:

A student asked a Zen Master, "If I work very hard, how long will it take for me to realize Zen?"

The Master replied,

"Ten years."

The student replied,

"If I work very, very hard, how long will it take for me to realize Zen?" The Master replied,

"Twenty years."

The student replied,

"If I work very, very, very hard, how long will it take for me to realize Zen?" The Master replied,

"Thirty years."

The student replied,

"But I don't understand.

Why does it take longer when I work harder?"

The Master replied,

"When you have one eye on the goal, you only have one eye on the path."

Too often in marketing we are obsessed with the goal to the point that we fail to understand that the path, procedures or the processes we used to reach the goal is equally, if not sometimes more, important.

We need do both—set the goals but also pay real importance to the strategies and tactics that will get us there over time.

Once you have a brand you have to manage it so that it accurately reflects who you and your company are over time. Brands, like people, have a past, present and future.

Brands evolve as people evolve, the good and the bad. Brands adjust when they extend into new products and services while shedding others that aren't growing or not as profitable as they once were. Tired brands gain a new edge by re-branding. Brands evolve because they need to respond to the competition. If you have a competitive advantage and are making money, competitors will try to capitalize on your brand by positioning their brand, products and services directly against yours.

And while you may have a first mover advantage, you will continually need to adjust and respond to the competition. Your brand needs to evolve as you and your business evolve. Perhaps you started out as a dentist, but now practice cosmetic dentistry. As you have become more successful, you have decided to donate some of your profits towards a social or environmental issue you are passionate about. All of these changes will affect your brand over time. Finally, I can only say that shit happens and there will be random acts and unintended consequences that may strike at the core of your brand at a moment's notice. These include unhappy employees, customers or something happens that shakes your brand and its reputation to the core. Stories, rumors, dissatisfied customers, etc. have a voice and move fast through social media. You need to look no further than the Malaysian Airline crashes, Carnival Cruise norovirus outbreaks and pink slime in beef to know how bad news or unwelcome news can damage a brand's image and reputation.

Managing And Protecting Your Brand's Online Reputation

"It takes 20 years to build a reputation and five minutes to ruin it. If you think about that, you'll do things differently." **- Warren Buffet**

Your brand is only as good as its reputation. We've all heard that phrase before; but, what does that really mean? And what is your online reputation? Your reputation forms as an intersection and interaction of three things. First – search engine results (both positive and negative), which rank your online profiles, press releases, interviews, social media updates, etc. Second – blogs and websites, where people may talk about your corporate or personal brand online. This can also come in the form of review sites. Finally – social media sites, where there are fans, mentions, likes, dislikes, etc. of your brand or business. Simply put, your reputation is the collection of shared and public info (data) about you and your brand put out by you, your competitors, enemies, customers, brand followers, brand haters, independent critics and reviewers.

This 'data' can be anything about any aspect of your brand or business, such as your customer service, the overall experience a customer has with you or the value and quality of your product, but it usually comes from specific points of influence such as:

- Consumer/product review sites (Amazon, Yelp, Google Plus/Places, ePinions, CitySearch, Better Business Bureau, Merchant Circle)

- Niche review sites (Angie's List, Zagat's)

- Search engines (Google People Search, Bing, Pipl, Spock, Facebook and 123 People)

- Blogging communities (Tumblr, Blogger, Wordpress, LiveJournal, Xanga, Open Diary)

- Social media networks (Facebook, Twitter, YouTube, LinkedIn, Flickr)

- Personal offline networks (e.g., TechCoast Angels, Kiwanis Club, Rotary Club)

- Research sites (Yahoo Answers, Quora, Rediff)

- Business research sites (Dun and Bradstreet, Hoovers)

- Personal information sites. There are sites out there that are in the business of collecting publicly available information and selling it. These include age, addresses, social security numbers, criminal records, liens, judgments, etc. They include Instant Checkmate, Spokeo, ZabaSearch, VitalRec and FirstGov)

- Social news and bookmarking sites (Digg, Reddit, Mashable, Stumbleupon, Technorati)

- Independent niche-related forums and online communities

- Other third party blogs and websites

- Word of mouth (the main offline source of reputation that usually ends up online in a review somewhere)

Reputations get built over time and evolve through four steps: establishing an online profile, identity development, reputation evolution and through the bestowment of trust.

This chart, by Laurel Papwoerth, illustrates this point in more detail:

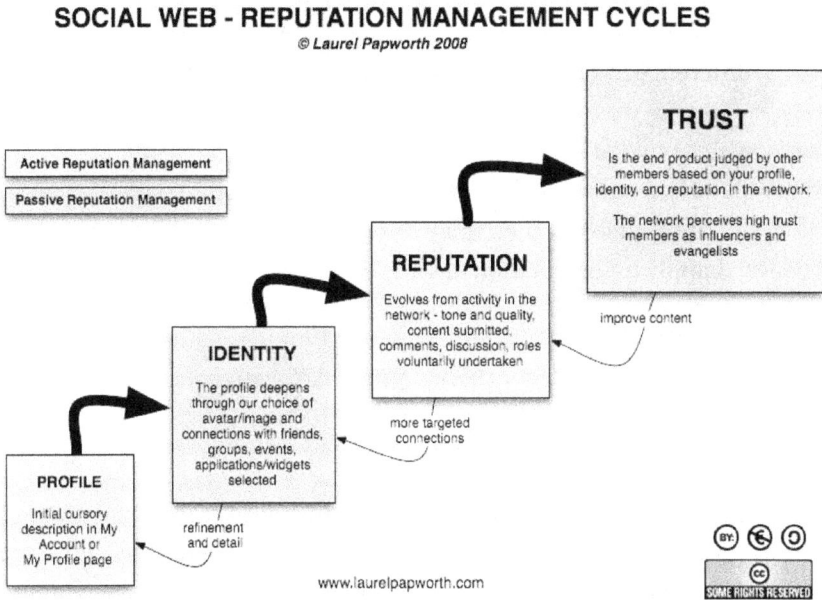

SOCIAL WEB - REPUTATION MANAGEMENT CYCLES
© Laurel Papworth 2008

Source:http://searchenginereputationmanagement.tumblr.com/
image/892021078

What people are saying about you and what you are saying about yourself all across these various online and offline platforms make up your brand's reputation. They must intersect positively and consistently to be impactful for your business.

It's what gives your potential new customers their first impression of you and it helps them decide if they should take the risk in doing business with you. Most people are using search online to check out you and your business online before doing business with you. In addition research has shown they are less likely to do business with you if they find negative information about you online. So you don't even see the business you are losing!

Here are some sobering facts ...

- 92% of Internet users read product reviews and 89% of people say that reviews influence their purchasing decisions. (eTailing Group)

- 73% of all activity online is in one way or another related to local content, activities or businesses. (Google)

- A difference of one star in an online review profile can lead to a 5–9% difference in revenues. (Harvard Business Review)

There's really only so much you can do to prevent someone trashing your online reputation, especially if someone just 'has it out for you'. Of course if it's defamatory or slanderous, there may be legal remedies against the person, but that doesn't apply to information already online. It is just not possible to get all of it removed.

But luckily there are a few things you CAN control:

What you put out there yourself

In other words, be careful what you post on your personal pages, blogs and social platforms if it can be in any way connected and traced to your business or brand. It's sad but true that your personal opinions, personality, tastes, ideas and thoughts will reflect back on your brand even if they are meant to be two totally different entities. It's just the way it is. So always make sure your personal private side matches your public side so you stay congruent with your message. Avoid questionable images. Stay away from talking about controversial subjects like sex, religion, politics, drugs, etc. The only caveat to this is if your business is about sex, religion, politics, drugs, etc. or your image is built on being a rebel and discussing controversial topics.

What you say/do in response to reviews and feedback

Most review places, blogs and social network sites allow you to reply to any comments or reviews left by customers. This is something you absolutely want and need to do, as long as it's done in a professional, civil and even kind-hearted way. You never want to attack someone even if they left a nasty review. Many times you can actually have the review or comment removed by the person who left it if you reach out to them, apologize and try to fix their issue in some way. Another way is to overwhelm the few negative posts with many more positive reviews.

Enlist your tribe and army to help you legitimately (and honestly) flesh out your online review locations with good words about you and your brand.

The customer experience you provide

You can prevent many negative reviews and comments just by offering stellar service and a one-of-a-kind customer experience. Establish and honor your guarantees, reply to all emails and phone calls quickly, handle things professionally and offer a great product/service for a great value. You want to be out on every social media platform that your audience is a part of. In addition, you should personally respond to comments, questions and address any issues or problems they may have in a quick and courteous manner. You also want to build a connection and bond and interact with your audience so their first experience (and all repeated experiences with you) is positive. The last thing you want is to push your brand, product or service all of the time. Sometimes – most of the time, actually – you need to be a leader, an authority, a teacher and a friend first. The sales and undying loyalty come later. And when it comes to reviews, even though you provide a great experience and stellar service, you'll still get negative feedback because sometimes you just have a bad day or something happens that's out of your control or maybe you just get a grumpy customer who isn't satisfied with anything. Don't worry too much as this is actually okay. One or two negative reviews are fine (and normal) as long as you have multiple positive ones to outweigh them. In fact, brands and companies with all positive reviews look suspicious and unnatural.

How easily the negative things about you can be found

There aren't many options to remove negative things about you or your brand online, but there are several ways to push them so far down in the search results or push negative reviews down to the bottom of the page. I'll teach you a few of these nifty techniques in just a bit.

Before I show you how to fix your online reputation, I want to tell you why it's important to make sure your online presence is both positive and strong. Proactively monitoring, caring for and cleaning your online reputation (like review sites and credit scores) can bring you a lot of important benefits, such as:

- Provide an early warning public relations system (if you see trouble brewing, you can stop it before it escalates).

- Keep your finger on the pulse (and thoughts) of your audience and then use those insights to improve your customer service, customer experience, products or services and your brand itself.

- Gain insights about your competitors (including what their customers think about them).

- Help you identify any weaknesses or gaps in your marketing or your products/services.

- Find new keywords or key phrases that your audience is using to search for your product/service or talk about your industry (such as on forums, in articles, on social media and blogs, etc.).

- Lower your internal and marketing costs by learning how to reach out to your audience more effectively and cheaply.

- Help to increase your traffic due to increased online visibility (which is always a great thing).

- Increase brand awareness and draw in new traffic.

- Increase your income potential by correcting problems or issues your customers currently have with your brand.

For me, though, the real kicker here is establishing an early warning system. If you keep tabs on your online reputation you can see patterns as they emerge in real time, listen in on conversations and get wind of any potential issues so you can address and correct them before they turn into public relation nightmares. This capability is truly pure gold for any brand.

There are tons of tools and methods online to do this. I want to shift gears now to show you how to handle any PR nightmares that may come your way.

What If The Worst Happens?

Because you know life is not perfect and bad things can and will happen, what do you do if the worst happens and you wake up one morning to find a potential or even full-blown public relations crisis on your hands?

It happens to the best of us and while it can often be prevented, sometimes you just get an awful customer or client or someone has a bad day and bad-mouthing your brand and trashing your reputation becomes their own personal stress-reliever.

What should you do?

- **Be prepared**

  You know it's bound to happen at some point and as they say, 'an ounce of prevention is worth a pound of cure.' In other words, have a crisis plan in place before the need for one arises. Start by monitoring all your social media properties daily so you are alerted to any changes or issues the moment they happen, whether it's a single unhappy customer or a massive customer outrage (think Chick-Fil-A, Abercrombie & Fitch or the recent rash of crazy employees doing disgusting things that are recorded and uploaded to YouTube such as Dominos, Subway and Taco Bell). Know who will be in charge of handling the emails, calls, social media posts and press. Decide what methods you will use to convey your message and what you will do if everything comes crashing down around you. Don't be caught with your proverbial pants down; have a social media crisis plan written and mapped out, just in case.

- **Identify the problem and communicate with your audience**

  The minute something happens, go to your employees and explain what just happened and let them know how you are handling it. Tell them what part they will play in crisis management and get them on your side. Next, address the public. Do a press release and video, put up a dedicated page on your site's home page about the issue and what you're doing to fix it and get on all your social platforms and start talking to your customers. Use social media to get your message across. Address every comment one by one, even if it's the SAME answer for each one. Communication is your number one weapon and resource. Apologies are more effective when they are done quickly and authentically. Finally, remember, repetition is a friend of communication.

- ### **Reach out to the movers and shakers first**

In every market there are influential people such as top reviewers, media, associations, power bloggers, press, Twitterers and even celebrities. You need to know who they are and how you can contact them in advance. If possible, you need to reach out right away to these movers and shakers and plead your case. If you can find allies in the influential social group leaders, you have a better chance of ending the crisis in a faster and more positive way. The key here is to already have a strong bond and relationship with these power-users before a crisis ever hits; that way, they will most likely be there for you when the shit hits the fan. If not, if you try to reach out to them after the fact, they may feel used and the backlash will be even worse.

Get comfortable with your skeletons

This may be a tough pill to swallow, but when a crisis hits, you need to be prepared and able to admit and openly discuss your skeletons – both current and past – personal and business - because they will come up. For example, if you were arrested or photographed for something a long time ago (e.g., DUI, love child, drug offense, topless in Europe), create a response to that issue before it surfaces. It is hard to argue with public records. Don't dodge the issues or the questions because if you do, you're just going to stir the pot even more and nothing will ever clear up and go away unless it's addressed. If you have criminal records, mug shots, etc. online, there are companies out there you can pay to have your online criminal records expunged. I cannot vouch for the effectiveness of these services as I do not have a criminal record I need to get rid of. These sites include the Fresh Start Law Center and Unpublished Mugshots.

Fix the issue

Don't just apologize ... explain what happened and how you plan to fix it or make it right. Do this right away and make sure each social media platform says the same thing. Also, keep in mind that people know how to get your attention if they feel you aren't giving it to them fast enough or fully addressing their concerns.

People are not above shaming you on a public forum to get your attention so be prepared to intercept this and deal with it immediately by giving a solution you can stick to. Finally, work with reputation management companies like Brandyourself.com and Reputation.com to bury negative search results into Google Search oblivion.

- **Update and respond continuously**

This is not the time to hide and avoid the press. Don't post once and run away from the issue. Update every social site, as well as your website, several times an hour. Stay on top of the communication and responses to your customers by email, phone and online – even if it takes your entire staff all day long.

- **Be transparent and own up to it**

If you messed up, don't deny it. Honesty is the best policy and people will respect you for standing up and taking the hit. Although I am not a lawyer (and this is not legal advice), you probably would want to consult with a lawyer, if owning up to something puts you in some sort of risk of criminal prosecution or civil litigation.

- **Know your story and get it out there**

Saying the wrong thing can be worse than saying nothing in a crisis. Make sure you have your story straight and all the facts are right. Make sure everyone is on board and stands behind what you are saying. Also make sure your story is coming from a person – a real human and not a logo or corporate identity. People don't trust corporations; they trust people. Have a pre-prepared 'fact sheet' and use it consistently across all media channels. Tell the same story and give the same message consistently to everyone. You don't want to be in the position of saying "what the Senator meant to say was ..."

- **Accentuate the positives**

While you don't want to be accused of misdirection, you need to draw as much attention back to the positive aspects of your brand as much (and as quickly) as possible. Be creative and look for ways to turn the crisis into an opportunity to promote a change agenda or an activism issue.

- **Consider humor (if appropriate)**

Sometimes the direness of a situation can be lessened with a touch of humor. Other times it will only make things much worse. For instance, if you made a boo-boo or did something embarrassing, humor could help. But if there's been a death or something tragic has happened, humor would not be appropriate. Just use your judgment and be sure to think it through before you make a formal statement.

- **Know when to keep quiet**

As I mentioned earlier, sometimes it may be best to stay quiet on certain issues. It's rare, but when it happens, you'll know if this is one of those 'speak out' or 'stay quiet' times. One of those 'stay quiet' times happened recently with the whole Paula Deen - Food Network debacle. People were posting like CRAZY on FN's social media sites, but FN declined to respond because they knew that getting involved in a racial debate was the last thing they needed and ultimately it would only make matters worse. Paula Deen's subsequent comments dug her in a deeper hole as well. They did what they felt they needed to do, gave their reasoning, stood by it and moved on in the hopes that everyone else would too ... eventually.

- **Check back post-crisis**

When the dust settles and things go back to a normal (or a semi-normal) state, don't let that be the end of it. The best way to ensure you're giving the best customer experience possible is to go back, check in and touch base with all those who issued complaints to see how they are doing and if they need any additional help or service. It means a lot to customers to know that you have the guts not only to admit when you are wrong, but also to make sure they are taken care even after the press has left and the crisis is over. That's when the real customer service and care begins.

Remember that a crisis can happen to anyone at any time, but it's rarely the end of the world if you are prepared for and handle it promptly and properly. Don't fear it and don't expect it, but still prepare for the worst just in case.

Benefits Of A Strategic Alliance Or Co-Branding Opportunity

Unless you own a walk-in retail business you are going to need to find partners (channels) to grow and expand your business over time. Partnership can have a lot of different meanings in a business context, from a channel to a business partner that splits the profits. When talking about brands and partnerships I prefer to use the terms 'co-branding' and 'strategic alliance'. In that case, what is a strategic alliance?

According to Wikipedia:

> *"A strategic alliance is a formal relationship between two or more parties to pursue a set of agreed upon goals or to meet a critical business need while remaining independent organizations."*

Investopedia says it's:

> *"An arrangement between two companies that have decided to share resources to undertake a specific, mutually beneficial project. A strategic alliance is less involved and less permanent than a joint venture, in which two companies typically pool resources to create a separate business entity. In a strategic alliance, each company maintains its autonomy while gaining a new opportunity. A strategic alliance could help a company develop a more effective process, expand into a new market or develop an advantage over a competitor, among other possibilities."*

Co-branding is actually a type of strategic alliance, but it's often used interchangeably even though it's not quite the same thing.

Wikipedia defines it this way:

> *"The term 'co-branding' is relatively new to the business vocabulary and is used to encompass a wide range of marketing activity involving the use of two (and sometimes more) brands. Thus co-branding could be considered to include sponsorships, where Marlboro lends it name to Ferrari or accountants Ernst and Young support the Monet exhibition. Co-branding is an arrangement that associates a single product or service with more than one brand name or otherwise associates a product with someone other than the principal producer. The typical co-branding agreement involves two or more companies acting in cooperation to associate any of various logos, color schemes or brand identifiers to a specific product that is contractually designated for this purpose. The object for this is to combine the strength of two brands, in order to increase the premium consumers are willing to pay, make the product or service more resistant to copying by private label manufacturers or to combine the different perceived properties associated with these brands with a single product."*

This kind of co-branding should not be confused with sponsorship, where a large company may have its logo on a race car or have a banner on the 50-yard line of a professional football stadium. There are several types of co-branding strategies that are most in common:

Ingredient co-branding: creating brand equity for materials, components or parts that are contained within other products. (e.g., Dell Computers with Intel processors or Betty Crocker brownies with Hershey's chocolate syrup.)

Same-company co-branding: when a company with more than one product promotes their own brands together simultaneously. (e.g., Kraft Lunchables with Oscar Mayer meats).

Brand licensing: an agreement where one company remits to another the use of the brand to apply to other products and services. For example in the comsumer camera space both Polaroid and Kodak license their brand names for camera-related products. Sharper Image is an example of another brand licensing firm.

Joint venture co-branding: two or more companies going for a strategic alliance to present a product to the target audience. (e.g. Fuji-Xerox, Worthington Ford and Target-Visa cards).

And finally, **multiple sponsors co-branding:** two or more companies working together to form a strategic alliance in technology, promotions, sales, etc. A great example is what the PGA does for its golf tours, with different companies sponsoring different holes like the Kodak Challenge.

To give you a better idea of what this looks like in the "real world," here are some examples of brilliant alliance, co-branding and partnership successes:

- Starbucks is literally the best at co-branding. They have aligned with Kraft to bring cold coffees into grocery stores, Barnes & Noble to create in-house coffee shops, PepsiCo to distribute and sell their Frappaccino even United Airlines to offer their coffee in branded logo cups on flights.

- Dell computers with OPI fingernail polish colors to bring 26 nail polish colors to their laptops

- Kellogg Pop-tarts combined with Smucker's fruit jam

- Citibank/American Airlines/Visa credit card partnership

- Duncan Hines 'Candy Shop' Brownies with Twix

- Marvel Comics and Visa recently co-developed a unique comic book addressing money management issues, starring The Avengers and Spiderman

- Martini Gold and Dolce & Gabbana have a long history of collaborations from martini bars in D&G clothing boutiques to a D&G suit line called Martini

- Pottery Barn began getting so many inquiries about what color paints were used in their catalogs that they partnered with paint company Benjamin Moore to create several different color palettes for their customers

- Naked Wines partnering with the Naked Chef (Jaime Oliver)

- Dairy Queen's Blizzards, for example, are co-branded with candy and cookie brands like Heath Bar and Oreo

- Kim Kardashian endorsing QuickTrim

- Disney's alliances with Mattel, McDonald's and Burger King

- Lexus GS 300 "Coach Edition" features the luxury Lexus sports-utility vehicle outfitted with Coach-branded leather upholstery and featuring the Coach logo on the floor mats and headrests. Some models even include a Coach leather weekend bag!

- Ford's 'Harley-Davidson Edition' truck and 'Eddie Bauer Edition' of the Ford Explorer

- Tide's retail laundry franchise

- HP Envy notebooks with Dr. Dre's 'Beats' audio software

- Apple and Nike teamed up to create NIKE + iPod Sports Kit

- Lays brand potato chips with KC Masterpiece barbecue sauce flavoring

Is it starting to sink in what this could mean for your brand? If not, let's look at the many awesome benefits co-branding and alliances can bring your brand. The rewards can be huge when you know what goals you want to accomplish beforehand and you have a strong partnering brand to help you achieve them.

Here are some of the awesome benefits from partnering with another brand:

- You can block a potential competitor threat by cornering the market with something so unique that they can't compete, especially if the goal is to combine forces in order to push another company out of the market completely.

- Whatever sparkle and shine is on your partner is now being shared by you and your brand. Brilliant and high quality by association.

- The more high quality, established and popular brands, associations, etc. you are connected to, the more popular and desirable you may appear in the eyes of the consumers. You can create a deeper impression and connection with your audience and their reputation and authority helps reinforce your brand's image more than your product alone would.

- Because your popularity and status increases, you have greater access to additional sources of funding, sponsorships press and investments.

- Expanding into new markets and customer targets will increase your customer base, sales revenues and royalty income.

- When two competent and responsible companies combine forces they can become more efficient and streamlined in their operations, finances and practices.

- Gives partner better and bigger marketing and exposure opportunities and wider coverage.

- Can create better innovation and creativity through collaboration that would not normally be possible with one brand alone.

- You can take advantage of an opportunity faster by leveraging the knowledge, resources and funding of another established brand.

- In the case of a scandal or problem, both brands split the blame and that can help tamper down some of the total backlash and heat.

- It's the best way to introduce and sell your products or services to the fanatics and loyal fans of another brand or market and get in on their 'halo of affection' that their fans feel for them (which is transferred to you by association).

- Build advantages of scale, scope and speed.

- Get better prices through bulk purchasing.

- Increase market penetration or market access.

- Enhance competitiveness in domestic and/or global markets, as well as product development

- Get access to new technology.

- Can help diversify and develop new business opportunities through new products and services.

- Accelerate research and development by sharing costs and resources.

- Increase the scale of your production output.

- It's a way to work together with other brands towards a common goal while not losing your individuality.

How To Know When A Strategic Alliance Is The Best Thing For Your Brand

I firmly believe almost any brand or business can benefit from a partnership, strategic alliance or a co-branding opportunity; however, just because you can it doesn't mean you should. It's more about timing, defining the benefit and getting incremental sales than anything else.

For example, is your market ready for what you are planning to bring to the table? Is your brand prepared for all the issues (such as growth, additional work, etc.) that come with a partnership? Is your partner in the best place and position possible to help you? Are you doing well enough right now without taking on new partnerships? Is your partner really the best option or are you settling because no one else will join you or the type of partner you really want doesn't yet exist?

These are all things you need to consider before you take the partnership plunge.

When I handled partnership marketing at HP and Kodak, I created this simple blueprint—well, more like a checklist or questionnaire—to help me decide if the partnership I was evaluating would be in the best interests of both parties:

1. Why do we want to partner with each other?

1. What specifically does the partnership do?

2. What is the end benefit – to the customer and each of the partners?

3. How does is it tie back to the company's strategy, business goals and market access?

4. How does the partnership strengthen the results of both companies? For example, I bring a product and you bring customer segment access to me that is one of my target markets.

2. What does each party bring to the table?

1. What specific capabilities or assets does each party bring to the table?

2. Who does what? How does the partnership translate into what each company brings, provides and has to do?

3. What investment dollars will each party bring to the table to launch the marketing alliance?

4. Is one party more dependent on the other, bringing more to the table, leading the alliance, etc.?

3. What does the end result look like?

1. Describe the successful partnership in 1-2 sentences.

2. What is the end game or result?

3. What does success look like? Financial, customer acquisition, revenue, etc.

4. What does the PR/messaging, strategy and content look like?

5. Is it a low key or 'Big Bang' alliance launch?

6. What is the partner commitment and effort going to be?

7. Does the sum of the parts lead to a better end result than going alone?

4. How do we each make money?

- How does each party derive a financial and/or market benefit from the partnership?

- Where does the benefit come from – a financial perspective, distribution perspective, market access perspective, brand building perspective? The possibilities are endless.

By carefully evaluating your win-win partnership approach you may give yourself and your brand additional competitive advantages and allow participation in markets where you did not have access.

Activating Your Networking Strategy

"... relationships take time; getting to know folks requires patience and people are generally cautious – if not fearful – of Johnny come lately that is asking, rather than giving." - **Jeremiah Owyang, Sr. Analyst at Forrester**

Now I must talk about the N word. Not *that* word. I mean the word <u>networking</u>. The word everybody loves to hate. An activity that is despised and maligned by many who have to do it. To be honest, I don't think many people really like networking. Once in a while I have my "game on" and I can be smooth as silk and talk to anybody about anything.

But for many of us it's not a comfortable activity; most people would call it a necessary evil to help move you, your business and your brand forward by connecting with other like-minded people. Some call it schmoozing and other people would call it a waste of time.

Yet it <u>is</u> the social lubricant of what makes businesses grow and brands standout. It can be done online and offline. When people talk about networking it can be fairly accurate to define it as "socializing for professional or personal gain."

But if you proceed just with this definition your networking activities will have limited success. The basic idea of networking is the concept of 6 degrees of separation and word of mouth advertising (WOMA). According to Wikipedia, "Six degrees of separation" is the theory that everyone and everything is six or fewer steps away, by way of introduction, from any other person in the world, so that a chain of "a friend of a friend" statements can be made to connect any two people in a maximum of six steps."

It was originally set out by Frigyes Karinthy and popularized by a play written by John Guare. By the way, through 23andme, a DNA service, I learned that many of you are probably 4th-6th cousins of mine ... so it works! (Hi, cousin ...).

With respect to WOMA people communicate with people who communicate with other people. They share information, both good and bad. And usually the message changes over time.

I have seen miraculous things happen in networking—wives who introduce their husbands who then go on to do a business deal or hire each other, people network their way into the company of their dreams because a friend of a friend knows the CEO, launches of personal brands with the most serendipitous encounters, etc.

You see networking is all about connecting _and_ making connections. Just like the eight arms of an octopus, those tentacles stretch out and touch or grab other things and those things touch more things and so on and so forth. Sometimes during this process the magic happens. You find connections and opportunities too good to be true. Serendipity? Possibly. Good timing or just plain luck may play a role.

The premier online tool for networking is LinkedIn and to a lesser extent other social media; but there are many other online and offline ways you can connect to build your network. For example, people join business groups like Rotary and Kiwanis clubs, country clubs, church groups, tips clubs, trade associations, university alumni groups, Toastmasters, Meetup groups, hobby associations, former company alumni, etc. and use those clubs as a way to start building their network while doing something they enjoy.

In order for networking to be successful, it must be purposeful and objective.

Although I often assume the role of a good Samaritan and help people that need it the most, I <u>focus</u> my networking on people who have the demographics and interests that allow me to expand my business in new ways and to build my brand.

My perspective of successful networking has a number of components and aspects:

Serving vs. Served - networking is all about helping and being in the service of others as your first foot forward. It is often called "paying it forward." This means that I am here to help you. If I gladly give my service through you, I will be rewarded later with things I can only imagine. This was the primary point in the book <u>The Secret</u> by Rhonda Byrne. And it has been called other names like "good karma", "random acts of kindness," etc. The purpose of networking is to help and not to sell. Popularized by the saying "what goes around comes around," a person's actions, whether good or bad, will often have consequences for that person. I believe this has been and will continue to be so true in my own life experiences. It also makes you feel good and takes you up a rung or two on the ladder of success. Try this experiment: next time you're on a toll road, pay the toll for the car behind you ... see how you feel. You can only imagine how the passengers of the other car will feel!

Cultivate Your Network — tend to your network like a farmer tends to his crops. This means engaging, responding and communicating with them in ways that keep the network alive and vibrant so people know your name and think about you for business opportunities, career moves and quality introductions. In theory stronger ties are preferable to weaker ties. Having said that, most of networking involves weaker ties; however, they can still provide numerous networking benefits and connections. If your network is larger than 100 people, you will have more weak ties than strong ones and that's okay—just know who is who and cultivate each accordingly as some weak ties can eventually become stronger over time and with nurturing, but you have to know when to let go and focus on the ones who can (and do) give you more of a return for your time, efforts and energy.

Engage the Network — networking isn't a spectator sport; it isn't something that you can watch from a distance and derive benefit. It's a dirty team sport, an in-your-face participant activity, not unlike a mosh pit I once had the pleasure of being in at a Bad Religion concert (true story). Now some of you will no doubt be uncomfortable with this idea. You believe you're an introvert, don't like to chit chat, have nothing valuable to say, don't like talking to strangers, etc. It's quite understandable. I'm confident that with some practice and tools you will be very functionally competent, if not an expert at it, despite the discomfort of actually doing it. Plus, it gets easier with time and experience and you may find yourself enjoying it! (Gasp.)

Frequency is Key — now I am not saying you need to go to every networking event out there. You can't! But part of the networking process is to choose the frequency and types of events you go to and groups you belong in. The more people and groups you connect with, the greater the value the network (and the networking) will be. But it is hard to know people in a large event. So beyond the large events, my preferred style of networking is a coffee meeting at Starbucks. Why? It has a limited duration (30-60 min), it's cheap (I always buy the coffee when I am doing the inviting) and it's simple to set up. I do these 1:1 meetings 10-15 times for every event I go to.

Online and Offline — If you are thinking that you can do all of your networking from behind a computer you would be dead wrong. While you can do some networking online using social media and email for some networking - face to face engagement is necessary and desirable. In fact, it's critical when it comes to building rapport and connection. If face to face is not possible because of distance, I recommend Skype or an old fashion phone call.

<u>Stay Open to the Possibilities</u> — I have met some incredible people through networking—artists, professionals, Ph.D. scientists, students, government workers, professors and executives. From each one I have met, I learned something from them and got more insight about myself or others. Some of these people have gone on to be in the 'inner circle' of personal and professional relationships I have established. Yes, networking can lead to friendships as well! To have this breadth of possibilities happen, it requires that you broaden your universe of activities in which you want to connect and be seen. At the same time, you need to make sure your network is compatible with your objectives. For example, you would not market your craft beer business at an Alcoholics Anonymous alumni meeting and scary, ghoulish Halloween costumes probably won't go well at your church's Harvest Festival.

<u>Don't Take it Too Seriously</u> — You're not going to mesh with everyone you meet and there are a lot of jerks out there who are not nice people and are sizing you up to see how high on the "help myself-o-meter" you score. Do not take this personally; it isn't about you so don't beat yourself up when it happens. And it will happen; so when it does, just move on. Some people are not going to want to help and are selfishly in it for themselves. Cross them off your lists. I like to look at networking as both a team sport and somewhat of a strategy game, like chess. I get a joie de vivre during the process. If I want to meet a CEO of a particular company, I will look at how I am connected to that person on LinkedIn and derive a strategy to get introduced. If I am not successful in one path I will look for another. I also don't let the 'gate keepers' tell me how to connect with their bosses. I am not working for them or their company. When meeting someone is a priority, think creatively for a way to stand out and get their (positive) attention – and don't take no for an answer. At the same time, don't be overtly pushy.

Examples of creative ways to do this are to meet them after they give a speech, send them 'snail mail' with an idea you think could help them or their company, join the charities they participate in or the causes they sponsor.

Network with a Purpose — Why are you networking? I hope it's not just because you have nothing else to do on a Wednesday evening. You need to have goals and objectives for your networking. You are spending time and money to do it so ... why are you doing it? Perhaps it's for a new job or to work in a new industry, expand your business connections, finds targets for your products and services, help you learn a new industry, gain new expertise, get new ideas, etc. The list is endless. At the same time, there are two things you should **not** use networking for:

> 1) ask for a job
> 2) try to make a sale.

Networking is not for those purposes. You may get a job or make a sale from networking, but that is not the goal of why you do it.

Go for Diversity and Size – Both are important, but you need a balance. The goal here is to have a variety of connections with different skills, positions, viewpoints, strengths, connections, contacts and industries so you have as many employment and partnership opportunities available to you as possible.

The Art of Networking - While there is some science behind networking, it is mostly an art. A learned one, to be sure – but if you talk to 100 different people about how to network properly, some general themes will emerge. You've heard this saying ... *"When it comes to looking for a job, it's not what you know, it's who you know."* Or *"it's not who you know, but who knows you."* Study after study confirms that ~70% of all jobs are found through networking. Networking can happen anywhere and come in all shapes and sizes when there are people that come together for a purpose. It can happen at school, work, neighborhood party, HOA meetings, churches, industry conferences/events, affinity groups, fraternities, airport gates, tradeshows, work, volunteering, your son's Boy Scout meeting, etc.

Don't procrastinate your networking, no matter how uncomfortable the idea feels to you. Just start doing it. Chinese philosopher Laozi (c 604 bc - c 531 bc), once said that "*a journey of a thousand miles begins with the first step.*"

Hence, even the most difficult and longest ventures have a starting point. So you need to start with that first step that will lead to success over time.

Goal-Setting And Contingency Planning

"Until it's over and done (This is it) One way or another (This is it). No one can tell what the future holds (This is it). Your back's to the corner (This is it). You make the choice of how it goes (This is it) The waiting is over." - **Kenny Loggins**

We've all done the New Year's Resolution thing where we write down a massive list of goals and plans for the upcoming year. While we get excited and inspired by the potential and opportunities that we feel await us now with this renewed vigor and vision we are endowed with, it always seems that in mere days or weeks we realize the only purpose of this list is to mock us and make us feel like useless smears of dog poop on the concrete of a New York back alley. At least that's how I feel when I can't seem to progress much less achieve even a fraction of what I set out to do. It should be easier and achievable.

Yes, missing goals and not making the progress you expected is part of human nature. It happens to all of us at one time or another.

We don't achieve those goals for many reasons, but three of the main ones are that we didn't set up the goals correctly, we had too many and we didn't have the true 'fire in the belly' passion and obsession behind them to make them happen.

But you're not going to make that same mistake with your brand and business goals, because I am not going to let you! In fact, I'm going to teach you one of the best ways to map out your goals so you can clearly focus your attention, take required and inspired action and track your progress every step of the way.

Before I do that, let's look at why goal-setting and goal-writing is so critical to your success. I've dug up a few studies I think will impress you:

Study 1

According to Dave Kohl, professor emeritus at Virginia Tech:

- People who regularly write down their goals earn nine times as much over their lifetimes as people who don't.

- 80% of Americans say they don't have goals.

- 16% do have goals but don't write them down.

- Less than 4% write down their goals and fewer than 1% review them on an ongoing basis.

Study 2

Psychology professor, Dr. Gail Matthews, of the Dominican University of California conducted a study on goals that included 267 participants from a wide variety of businesses organizations and networking groups throughout the United States. The results of her study were "Share your goals with a friend" and this is what she found:

People who wrote down their goals, shared this information with a friend and sent weekly updates to that friend were on average 33% more successful in accomplishing their stated goals than those who merely formulated goals.

Study 3

A study was done on why 3% of Harvard MBAs make ten times as much as the other 97% combined and they found the answer to be a rather simple question: "Have you set clear, written goals for your future and made plans to accomplish them?" The interviewers asked new graduates from the Harvard's MBA Program and found that:

- 84% had no specific goals at all

- 13% had goals but they were not committed to paper

- 3% had clear, written goals and plans to accomplish them

In 1989, the interviewers again interviewed the graduates of that class. You can guess the results:

The 13% of the class who had goals were earning, on average, twice as much as the those individuals who had no goals at all.

Even more staggering – the three percent who had clear, written goals were earning, on average, ten times as much as the other 97 percent put together.

How's that for persuasive data on the benefits of setting and writing out your goals? There's not much more I can add to that, so let's move on to the "how."

How To Write Powerful And Effective Goals You Can Actually Accomplish

We've talked at length in previous chapters about your vision and the BHAGs (Big Hairy Audacious Goals) for your brand, so here is where you do the footwork to make those actually happen.

Now there are literally hundreds of books, blogs and even courses that focus on the topic of goal-setting out on the market. I'm not going to write a book here or reinvent the wheel, because you can always go and do your own research if you feel inspired. All I'm putting down here is MY personal 6-Step Process that helps me get what I want in my life and for my brand.

6 Steps To Setting And Achieving Your Goals

1. Start With The Most Important Or Critical Goals First.

Studies have shown that our brains can only focus on three to five things at any one time, so if you overwhelm yourself with a page and a half of goals, you're already setting yourself up for failure. You don't need to address or even start on every goal at once, so choose the one or two most urgent and pressing goals, most important goals or a mix of those and a few easier, shorter term goals.

What it really comes down to is ROI – which goals will grow your brand, increase your income, improve your skills, make your life and your job simpler, easier and more enjoyable and which ones will produce the biggest and best results? Or which goals would solve a problem or fix a critical issue in your brand? When in doubt, start with those first. If not, it's kind of like knowing you have a room full of rotting trash that badly needs to be taken out before rats and flies take over, but you decide to organize your sock drawer and polish the silverware instead. It just doesn't make any sense.

Of course, if you are a tragically disorganized person or have some attention-deficit disorder and you know it's affecting your productivity, clarity and income, then adding an organizationally-focused goal to your list would be a huge benefit and ROI to you and your brand. On the same note, if one of your goals is a biggie with a bunch of steps and processes needed to accomplish it, doing these small things will get you to the end result and wouldn't be considered a pointless task. Your intuition will let you know what is what, so don't worry. You'll instinctively know what small tasks are parts of a bigger main goal and what tasks are just pointless time-consumers.

What you want to avoid is starting with or only working on the little, almost pointless goals that don't make a dent in your overall vision output or income.

So, before you start any goal-setting process or method, make a list of ALL your goals and rank them in order of importance, urgency and ROI. Create the realistic steps that will allow you to cross the three to five sub-goals that will give you your big goal achievement. That way you'll have them ready and will know which ones to focus on first during the upcoming exercises. And don't worry about refining and defining them – we'll do that in just a bit.

2. Work SMARTer, Not Harder

By smarter, I mean by using the SMART Goals system for defining and achieving goals. SMART is an acronym that has various meanings depending on who you ask, but the one I follow is Specific, Measurable, Action-Oriented, Realistic and Time-Bound.

Here's how to make SMART goals:

S

Specific
State exactly what you want to achieve. Can you break a larger task down into smaller items?

M

Measurable
Establish clear definitions to help you measure if you're reaching your goal.

A

Action-Oriented
Describe your goals using action verbs, and outline the exact steps you will take to accomplish your goal.

R

Realistic
Give yourself the opportunity to succeed by setting goals you'll actually be able to accomplish. Be sure to consider obstacles you may need to overcome.

T

Time-Bound
Now much time do you have to complete the task? Decide exactly when you'll start and finish your goal.

Source: http://hlwiki.slais.ubc.ca/images/thumb/6/6c/Smart_goals_1.jpg/240px-Smart_goals_1.jpg

3. Write Your Goals Down On Paper

This is essential to your success. You can't leave them in your head and expect them to simply come to life. There is immense power in writing down your goals, even if you never go any further than that (which of course you should to ensure they actually happen). Post them somewhere and look at them every day.

When you write something down, you are stating your intentions and setting things in motion. You are telling yourself that you place a high enough priority on this goal that you are willing to not only think about it, but also write it down clearly and concisely.

Think of it this way – you have millions of thoughts going in and out of your mind all day and you rarely pay attention to more than a handful.

And even those you tend to forget if you're not constantly feeding them with attention, emotion and focus. So the only way to prove to yourself that a goal is more than just a passing thought—that it is indeed, something of vital importance to you and has passion, meaning and purpose—you must take that extra step and write it down.

4. Take Inspired Action

Having a goal is not the same thing as achieving it. This is a distinction that we all already know, but here's the thing ...

We may know it, but often just the act of writing down a goal is fulfilling enough – gives us a sense of accomplishment and pride – that we tend to stop there. We sit back, smile and revel in the glory of making it this far. Trust me, is a feat in its own right. But if you stop there and you let the satisfaction of writing your goals eat into the passion and obsession for actually achieving your goals, you'll never get any further than where you are right at this very minute.

You'll never feel the REAL accomplishment and pride that comes when you look back on a list of five goals you started – and finished.

Don't fall for that false sense of accomplishment. Don't procrastinate. Acknowledge your success in getting this far and then immediately move on to the steps you need to accomplish to achieve each of these goals. Make a list of every tiny little action that needs to happen along the way to each goal, in order to get to that goal.

For example, if your goal is to go shopping at Best Buy, you don't just think "I want to be in Best Buy" and suddenly you're there! You have to first make the decision to go, get dressed, grab your wallet (or purse), get your keys, lock the door to the house as you leave, get in the car, start the car, check for gas, put on your seat-belt, pull out of the driveway and start your journey. Then you have stoplights/stop signs to pass through, traffic to watch out for and very specific roads to follow in order to get there. Then you still have to find a place to park before you can get out and go to the store.

Yes that's a bit over-detailed, but I hope you see my point. Your goal is your destination and there will always be a series of smaller actions you need to take in order to get from where you are now to where you want to be. You would have never arrived at Best Buy if you had not first made the decision to go and then taken all the necessary actions and path to get there.

5. Revisit and Review

What good is a grocery list that you never look at? What point is it to have a $150 day planner if you don't bother opening it daily to see your schedule? Having a list of goals is great, but reviewing and tracking them on a regular basis is where the magic happens. Then you can see how you are doing, tell if you're off track and adjust your trajectory based on any growth or changes in your business situation.

When you review your goals, always ask yourself "what is the NEXT step I need to take in order to achieve this goal?" Equally important is to under-stand what actions need to take place to get to the next step. This will help you make sure you are always taking the next step and going in a forward progressive motion to accomplish your goals, even if it's tiny baby steps. These 'next steps' – no matter how small – are the ones that need to be added to your daily 'to-do' list so you can always be moving in the right direction. It's up to you whether you review them daily or weekly, but don't put them off more than a week.

6. Be Careful Who You Share Your Goals With

I know you're excited about where you see yourself and your brand in the upcoming months and years and the vision you have about your success may be barely contained. But here are two reasons why you may want to consider keeping your goals to yourself (or only share it with a chosen few):

- Talking too much about your plans, vision and goals could actually drain the life and creativity out of them and leave you feeling drained and uninspired. It can even contribute to feeling satisfied just by talking about it rather than doing it. It really is as undesirable as it sounds when it comes to achieving your goals.

- If you share your vision or goals with someone that doesn't approve, doesn't believe you can do it or is jealous of you, then you risk their negativity and bad mojo or vibes contaminating your own passion and drive. You may find yourself second-guessing or trying to change to accommodate or suit them. You may lose faith in yourself or go off-track chasing something that's not what you really wanted in the first place.

The only people that should know about your goals are those that are directly responsible for helping you achieve them, as well as your support team, partner or Mastermind group. The key is that they support you 100% both verbally and with their actions, as well as have faith you can do it. If not, they don't need to know. Focus less on 'telling' and more on 'doing'.

Goal-setting has so many benefits, but it all starts with one single step – that one action of asking yourself, "where am I now, where do I want to be, what do I need to do to get there and by when?"

Growth, Adaptation, Improvement And Repetition

Let me now shift to talk about growth and evolution of a business and brands. And no, I'm not talking about the creationist vs. evolutionist theory. I'm speaking about the growth and adaption all businesses need to have in order to be successful over the long term.

The basic principle here is that businesses evolve, change and adapt, based on changes in their environment and their level of success. Only the best and strongest survive and adapt. As a human, a brand and a business, you are never at a 100% stable point. You're either evolving or devolving – there are no in-between states (even though you may feel your business is at status-quo, not growing or declining). I am sure Neanderthals thought that as well, just before they died out to the superior Modern Man.

Change is a continuous process based on your goal-setting, environmental factors and the expected/actual results of your business. And businesses and brands that evolve and change over time are more likely to be successful because they are able to be flexible, responsive and adaptable to any circumstance that comes along.

Think about the recession we have been in since 2007 and the slow recovery. In a good economy lots of marginal businesses succeed because there's great economic demand. In a bad economy marginal businesses fail and the ones that survive adapt to the changes and evolve. Of course, having a high-quality, differentiated brand and business also helps!

Here's a great diagram about the change process all brands and businesses must go through at some point in order to stay relevant and successful:

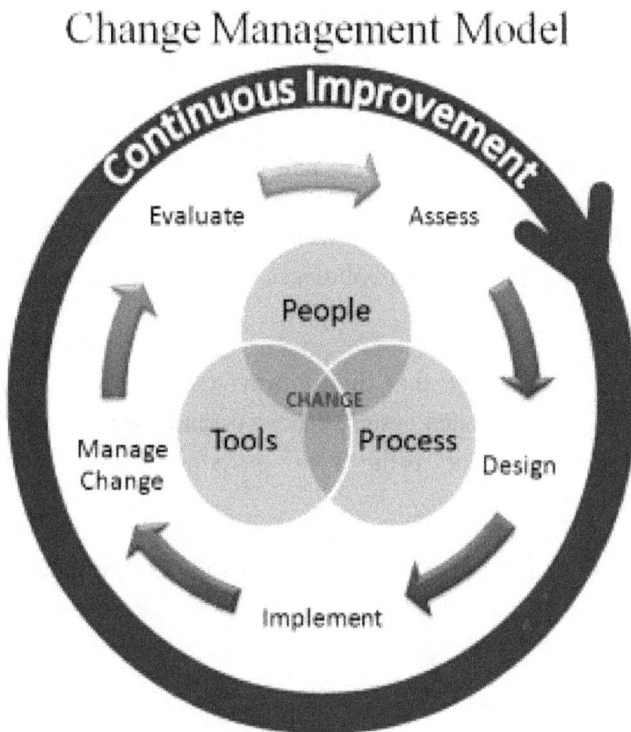

Change Management Model

Continuous Improvement

Evaluate   Assess

People

CHANGE

Tools   Process

Manage Change   Design

Implement

Source: http://planzsolutions.com/change management model png.png

We know from research that over 500,000 new start-ups are born every year in the US alone. Of that, 50% are likely to fail within the first year. Within the first five years another 50-80% are expected to fail. There are many reasons for this including a bad economy, lack of funding and lousy business ideas or structures; however, another big reason is a business' inability to adapt to changes and become fluid and flexible.

Over and over I've seen how businesses that adapt and change are much more likely to stay in business than those who fight tooth and nail to stay the same as they have always been.

I'm here to tell you that no business is too big to fail or too small to succeed. Let's look at companies like Kodak, Borders or Blockbuster. They failed because they were unable to adapt to the market disruptions in their business, mostly because digital delivery of content was disrupting their bricks and mortar retail storefronts. However, companies in the same industries like Fuji Film, Barnes and Noble and Netflix have survived and thrived.

Why? Because they anticipated change and adapted their businesses (and business models) to the realities of the new marketplace.

Continuous improvement requires a feedback loop that continually evaluates, assesses, designs, implements and manages the change that is derived from the process.

It's important to note here that this improvement process has components of people and other financial assets, processes and tools. I often refer to the interaction of these elements as the 'business system'.

What do I mean by system here? A *system* is a repeated course of action – a way of doing things – that brings about a desired result. The combination of people, time, money, tools, systems and the processes used to manage the business can have a great impact on the ability of businesses to adapt, evolve and improve over time.

> **Note:** *I once interviewed for a job where the same people were managing the same business, in the same way, for the last 20 years. For them, change was disruptive. They were unable to see the positive*

outcomes of continual improvement. I'm glad I didn't take the job because I could see far enough down the road to know that if they didn't break their old rigid habits and become more fluid and flexible, they wouldn't survive very long at all!

A big part of the business system is setting up repeatable processes and automating the business so you can check and measure how you're doing along the way. If you have processes and tools that can scale as your business grows you'll be better prepared to adapt and respond to the changes you're likely to encounter.

> **Note:** *Some definitions need to be made here just so we're all on the same page. When I talk about people I mean permanent hires, contractors, virtual assistants, outsourcing, etc. When I talk about processes I mean the methods and established procedures you have in place for key parts of the business. For example, revenue forecasting, scheduling, pricing or product launches. When I speak about tools I mean the resources you have in place to help you measure your performance or automate key processes. Examples could include Google Analytics, automated email responders, domain hosting, database management and the like.*

Keep in mind that no entrepreneur gets it exactly right on the first try, which is why starting a business or building a brand is such an iterative, discovery-based process. Through each business cycle you will learn something new and modify the business model a bit. Business assumptions change and your business will change as you will learn more about the customers and niche you serve.

This is called "pivoting," where the business model is modified when a hypothesis proves invalid. This does not mean that one failure results in a completely new vision. It just means taking stock of everything and adjusting the strategy and plan accordingly.

PDSA – The Continuous Improvement Method

A really good way to plan for continued improvement, growth and adaptation is to use the Plan-Do-Study-Act framework created by W. Edwards Deming (originally called the Plan-Do-Check-Act or the Deming Wheel). It was embraced whole-heartedly by Japanese companies and was the basis for the rise of companies like Toyota, Sony, Canon and Fujitsu in the last 50 years.

The PDSA method is a simple yet effective way to solve problems, test new ideas and manage change in a variety of areas, from quality control and marketing to new product/service creation.

The cycle consists of:

> **PLAN** - Clearly identify the problem so you can address it and map out a plan of attack.

> **DO** - This is not where you actually implement the new process or idea completely. It just means you try it (test it out in a small way) so you can then move on to the next step.

> **STUDY** - Study the data and make any changes needed before implementing the idea.

> **ACT** - Once you have everything the way you want it you can now fully implement the entire polished solution or idea in its final stage.

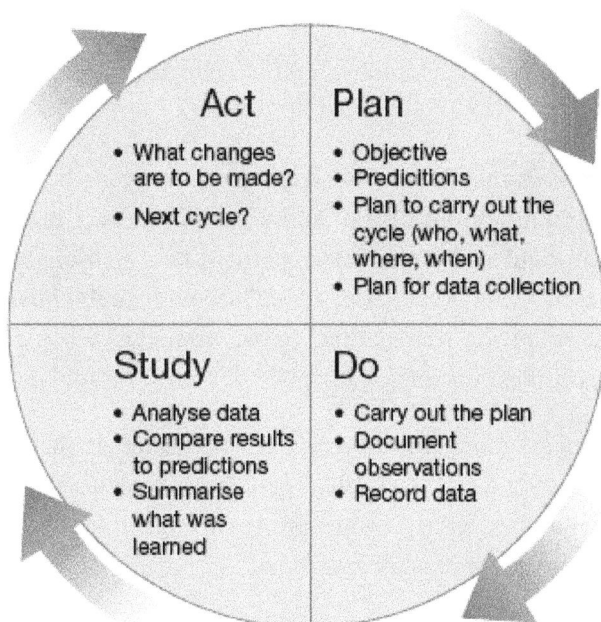

Sources: Deming, W.E.: Out of the Crisis. Massachusetts Institute of Technology, Cambridge 1982, S. 88.http://www.stritch.luc.edu/lumen/MedEd/softchalkhdht/CMEFacDevWebPage/Plan.gif

So when it comes time to try out something new or when you're facing a problem you don't know how to solve or you just want to make sure you're using the best possible method for the situation, call up the PDSA process and apply it to whatever you're dealing with. It's such a powerful and effective system that even the National Health Service (U.K.) and many other health organizations and professionals use it on a regular basis to streamline their methods, test out new ideas and policies, problem-solve and just get organized.

Rinse and Repeat

We've all heard the expression "lather, rinse and repeat" and while it started out as a humorous phrase on your shampoo bottle (presumably to use more), it's made its way into marketing and business where it often means just systematically following instructions or procedures without any critical thought or real reason.

But it also has a more metaphorical meaning. Let me explain ...

Thomas Edison once said, *"I have not failed. I've just found 10,000 ways that won't work."*

What this means is that as you establish and grow your business, there will always be a certain amount of trial and error that occurs in order to get the business model right and operating smoothly like a well-oiled machine. This is why many franchises are so successful. Once you get the business right and revenue starts following it is natural to ask yourself, *"How do I apply this success in my business expansion plans?"*

So in this instance, 'lather, rinse and repeat' can mean that once you have found what works and you have established business processes in place, you keep doing it over and over again. If you want to increase the results, you increase the frequency or amount of what is working.

For example, if I get 100 new customers a month that pay me $100 each, I earn $10,000. If I work harder and get 200 new customers a month, I make $20,000 a month, assuming I have a repeatable business and put in the time and resources to double my business. However, it also means that once you establish your niche and your brand (and are successful in it), you begin to think about how to expand your business and business model into adjacent markets and opportunities. Adjacent markets are often the best answer when a business is faced with the question of "what's next?" How do you take the business success you have in one niche and duplicate it in a similar, adjacent market opportunity?

Those are sweet spots where companies can bring solutions and systematized processes and technologies developed for one set of customers and apply them to a new but similar customer or market. This is a huge opportunity for you and your business and brand. So how do you do that?

Geoffrey Moore in the book, *Crossing the Chasm*, talks about this concept as a set of bowling pins in a Bowling Alley. The idea is that business is like a triangular formation of bowling pins. If you hit the first pin it knocks down adjacent pins and so on and so forth.

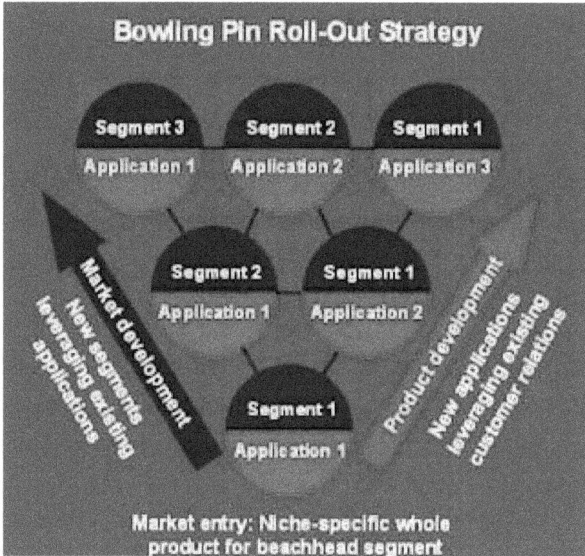

Source: http://www.caneval.com/vision/venturing.html

The strategy in the bowling alley is this:

Instead of wanting to move the entire herd at the same time, attempt to move multiple, smaller herds.

Here is the place where you could get small populations excited and conversing about your brand, product or service. When you have successfully penetrated one niche, expand to another related one with the same business system.

Here are some great examples:

1. Your internet marketing business focused on dentists, expands to other professions like a medical doctor, lawyer or accountant.

2. The franchise model. You successfully build a product or service in one geographical market and expand it to other regional markets (Think McDonalds, Sports Clips and Jiffy Lube).

3. Your successful general dentistry practice evolves to offer easy credit payments or cosmetic dentistry to a new set of patients.

4. Your Mercedes-only car repair service is replicated to other German car imports like BMW, Porsche and Audi.

5. Your experience as a CEO in one industry extends into other industries or the non-profit space.

In summary, once you have figured out how to make money with your brand and business (in your niche), you should rinse and repeat specific aspects of your business to new customers in order to maximize profits and improve the chances of additional successful outcomes.

One tactical example is to continue to use or re-use successful marketing programs that are driving your brand to more leads and sales. If you have figured out a way to drive traffic and conversions for your business, do it again or mix things up with your successful campaign as the platform.

The second thing is to expand that business to adjacent markets that can use the same business models and systems you created for your original business. Discard the parts of the business that are not making you money and amplify those parts of the business that are working well. It's downright brilliant when you think about it. Also, you should try to automate as much of the business as you can, so you can make money even when you sleep.

Let me conclude with the 10 Commandments for Continuous Improvement. Kaizen is the practice of continuous improvement in manufacturing.

It was originally introduced to the West by Masaaki Imai in his book Kaizen: The Key to Japan's Competitive Success in 1986. This is just some food for thought before we part:

1. Open mind to change.
2. Think yes we can, if.
3. Attack process, not people.
4. Seek simple solutions.
5. If it's broken, stop to fix it.
6. Use creativity, not capital.
7. Problems are opportunities in disguise.
8. Find the root cause – why, why, why.
9. Use wisdom of the many, not knowledge of one.
10. There is no final destination on the improvement journey.

In Closing

Before we conclude, just take a moment to reflect back at your journey. I hope you now have a higher level of clarity, vision, passion and knowledge about your brand that you didn't have before – and it's all yours. You did it. Your blood, sweat, tears and vision. Now you're almost there; you can see the finish line, the cheering crowds, the sparkling trophy of success and the feeling of elation and pride that comes from achieving something this precious and desirable.

However, just because you've worked hard doesn't mean that in this last step of the process you can rest on your laurels and take it easy. You may be nearly done with this particular run of knowledge, but you're nowhere near done in your journey for success, wealth and thirst for learning and experience.

In fact, if I ask you the rhetorical question, "are we done now?" The answer is emphatically "no, you are not done. You're never done!"

All of the work you have done is merely a snapshot in time. Just like a photograph, we age and grow in real life (hopefully for the better) and like clothing and hairstyles, your brand will change as well over time. If you have done all of these previous exercises, then you have already built the foundations of a new, solid brand. But when building a majestic cathedral you never stop at just the foundation. Furthermore as a majestic cathedral ages, it will need renovation.

It must evolve and grow. YOU must evolve and grow. You must execute your brand and continuously revise your brand and its marketing over time.

Why? Because the world, your business *and* your competition are constantly changing. S.T.A.R.™ branding is all about having a standout, differentiated brand. If you discover a niche in which people see you are successful, you will attract competitors who will enter your market and try to make money off of your ideas and value proposition. You need to look at your brand and think about how it and your business will expand, grow and evolve in a way that keeps you one step ahead over time.

As we end this final step of our branding process, let me leave you with a few, final thoughts about branding.

1. Branding is a journey, destination, journey, destination, etc.; it evolves over time as you, your competition and business evolve.

2. Great brands have a deliberate purpose and vision.

3. Awesome brands stand out with bold value and differentiation, which is much better than commoditization, the state most brands are in. This requires creating and delivering a customer experience that is better than and differentiated from your competitors.

4. Your brand needs to be an extension of you. If it doesn't feel right, it isn't right.

5. You must understand your brand is a realistic view of who you are. If you don't believe your brand to be true, how do you want others to believe in it?

6. Declare and own your brand identity, personality and promise with conviction.

7. Brand building takes time and must be measured over months and years for growth and goal achievement.

8. Branding is all about being deliberate, consistent, authentic, strategic and differentiated. Always be ready to "promote the value" of your brand.

9. Half the battle is showing up and having a world-class brand. The other half is about commitment, dedication, inspiration and perspiration in going the last mile and closing the sale.

10. Brands are never secure in their awareness, preference and value. They are always declining or increasing in these attributes. There is no steady state or equilibrium. Don't fall into that trap! Therefore, you need to address and manage your brand on a continuing basis.

11. In order to be a successful leadership brand, you must have authority, expert status, credibility, trust, stamina, social proof and influence.

12. Great brands always practice thought leadership by giving away their best ideas and thoughts in the form of valued content. This is "the what" of the business. Successful brands monetize the value of their knowledge and expertise with "the how."

13. Great brands always over deliver on value and customer experience. This engenders brand loyalty.

14. A brand's visual identiy must reflect what the company <u>and</u> customer want to see and need in a logo or brand mark.

In conclusion, will there be challenges along the way? Of course there will be. Don't let that stop you from taking action. Turn problems into possibilities and obstacles into opportunities.

The content and insights I have given to you have led to the success of many companies and businesses that have sold billions of dollars of goods and services.

It's hard work, but with effort and time, I'm very confident you will be able to build your SuperS.T.A.R.™ brand.

Finally, don't forget to register to get a couple of bonus tools and exercises. If you want to go much deeper on these topics or get some personal coaching from me, please visit the BRAND TO SELL™ program site at <u>http://www.mybrandtosell.com</u>.

REGISTER

This book for more content

(Videos, Special Reports, etc.)

at:

BrandtoSellBook.com

Links Referenced In
Book For Print Readers

If you purchased the print version, some of the embedded web links were not included unless they were specifically called out.

Therefore, I am publishing this list of all of these links listed in this book. Please remember that some links may change over time.

Chapter 1

- http://www.vincentferraro.com/
- http://www.mybrandtosell.com/
- http://www.wikid.eu/index.php/Brand
- https://twitter.com/ryanmorse33/status/469934009594957824/photo/1
- http://business.usi.edu/dean/2011spr-cob.aspx
- http://thenextweb.com/entrepreneur/2011/05/25/the-9-types-of-online-business-models- which-one-do-you-use/
- http://smallbusiness.chron.com/list-business-models-338.html
- http://www.businessmodelgeneration.com/downloads/business_model_canvas_poster.pdf
- https://commons.wikimedia.org/wiki/File:SWOT_en.svg
- http://www.semrush.com/

Chapter 2

- http://www.taliesin.edu/sheltersmain.html
- http://jsahni.blogspot.com/2014/02/2014-new-whole-product.html
- http://businessmodelgeneration.com/canvas/vpc?_ga=1.178151653.1584174714.1442271356
- http://torgronsund.com/2011/11/29/7-proven-templates-for-creating-value-propositions-that-work/
- https://marketingcampaigndevelopment.wordpress.com/2009/12/08/do-we-really-need-a-positioning-statement/

- http://thesocializers.com/thearchetypes/
- http://www.storybranding.com/site/
- http://thesocializers.com/thearchetypes/
- http://www.scielo.br/scielo.php?script=sci_arttext&pid=S1807-76922012000200004
- http://pivotcon.com/how-the-big-five-personality-traits-impact-your-brand-community/
- http://facultyfiles.deanza.edu/gems/abrahamsmatt/TheBrandCalledYou.pdf
- http://en.wikipedia.org/wiki/Monomyth
- http://www.hotsauceworld.com/wafuupco1l.html
- http://www.buttpaste.com/
- https://www.google.com/h?q=funny+brand+names+around+the+world&tbm=isch&tbo=u&source=univ&sa=X&ei=5I2GUoylLs3q2wXc3YDYBA&ved=0CC4QsAQ&biw=1406&bih=775
- http://www.taglineguru.com/sloganlist.html
- http://www.noesismarketing.com/building-a-brand-pyramid/
- https://www.fiverr.com/
- http://www.logoworks.com/
- http://99designs.com/
- http://collectiveindustries.co.uk/8998/branding-colour-psychology/

Chapter 3

- http://www.jaredcorcoran.com/brandidentity-worksheet
- http://blogs.wsj.com/law/2011/11/02/law-blog-fireside-vince-ferraro-the-guy-trying-to-occupy-the-occupy-trademark/
- http://www.mybrandtosell.com/
- http://www.redapples.com/
- http://www.paper.li/
- http://www.cisco.com/web/strategy/docs/education/Multimodal-Learning-Through-Media.pdf
- http://www.istockphoto.com/
- http://www.depositphotos.com/
- http://www.123rf.com/

- http://www.dailyblogtips.com/how-to-create-a-favicon/
- http://themeforest.net/
- http://www.woothemes.com/
- http://www.elegantthemes.com/
- http://www.rockettheme.com/
- http://whatwpthemeisthat.com/
- http://wix.com/
- http://web.com/
- http://en.wikipedia.org/wiki/Customer
- http://en.wikipedia.org/wiki/Supply_chain
- http://en.wikipedia.org/wiki/Good_(economics)
- http://en.wikipedia.org/wiki/Service_(economics)
- http://en.wikipedia.org/wiki/Customer_relationship_management
- http://www.expertprogrammanagement.com/2011/06/customer-marketing-and-relationship-management-currys-pyramid/
- http://openmarketing.com/blog/for-b2bs-smbs-the-oscar-for-best-social-medium-goes-to-twitter/
- http://www.warriorforum.com/ad-networks-cpa-cpm-cpl-millionaire-makers/606037-list-paid-traffic-sources.html
- http://www.toolsformoney.com/financial_planning_prospecting_and_practice_management.htm
- http://www.amazon.com/Influence-Psychology-Persuasion-Business-Essentials/dp/006124189X/ref=sr_1_1?s=books&ie=UTF8&qid=1383006973&sr=1-1&keywords=robert+cialdini
- http://www.amazon.com/NLP-Essential-Guide-Neuro-Linguistic-Programming/dp/0062083619/ref=sr_1_2?ie=UTF8&qid=1383007200&sr=8-2&keywords=NLP
- http://cdn2.hubspot.net/hub/53/file-13222290-pdf/docs/ebooks/original files/hbebook20120307.pdf
- http://www.comscore.com/Insights/Press_Releases/2013/6/comScore_Releases_May_2013_U.S._Search_Engine_Rankings
- http://moz.com/beginners-guide-to-seo
- http://www.lynda.com/SEO-training-tutorials/1469-0.html
- http://training.seobook.com/
- https://www.udemy.com/seo-training/

- https://adwords.google.com/o/Targeting/Explorer?__
  c=1000000000&__u=1000000000&ideaRequestType=KEYWORD_
  IDEAS
- http://www.xml-sitemaps.com/
- http://www.google.com/webmasters/
- https://blog.serps.com/how-to/setup-google-authorship/
- http://www.searchenginejournal.com/new-moz-study-shows-
  correlation-between-google-1s-and-high-rankings/67801/
- http://searchengineland.com/seotable/
- http://www.wordstream.com/blog/ws/2013/05/29/what-is-
  Inbound-marketing%23.
- http://www.pamorama.net/2013/07/13/5-content-curation-
  infographics/
- http://itwofs.com/beastoftraal/2011/02/04/social-media-
  engagement-5-cs-to-use-content-to-your-advantage/
- http://copyscape.com/
- http://contentmarketinginstitute.com/2012/11/2013-b2c-consumer-
  content-marketing/
- http://wronghands1.wordpress.com/
- http://conversationprism.com/
- http://conversationprism.com/wp-content/uploads/2014/11/
  ConvoPrismLarge.jpg
- http://www.lumapartners.com/resource-center/lumascapes-2/
- http://static2.businessinsider.com/
  image/4fb5077becad045f47000003/this-insane-graphic-shows-how-
  ludicrously-complicated-social-media-marketing-is-now.jpg
- http://www.ebizmba.com/articles/social-networking-websites

Chapter 4

- http://searchenginereputationmanagement.tumblr.com/
  image/892021078
- http://www.businessnewsdaily.com/7901-best-reputation-
  management-services.html
- http://freshstartlawcenter.
  com/?gclid=CNvBvszPtboCFStgMgodphMAuw

- http://www.unpublishmugshots.com/
- http://www.reddit.com/r/technology/comments/j1mit/how_to_ remove_yourself_from_all_background_check/
- https://www.distilled.net/blog/reputation/reputation-101-how-to- protect-your-brand-online/
- http://www.amazon.com/The-Secret-Rhonda-Byrne/ dp/1582701709/ref=sr_1_1?ie=UTF8&qid=1375632926&sr=8- 1&keywords=the+secret
- http://en.wiktionary.org/wiki/Laozi
- http://hlwiki.slais.ubc.ca/images/thumb/6/6c/Smart_goals_1. jpg/240px-Smart_goals_1.jpg
- http://planzsolutions.com/change management model png.png
- http://www.stritch.luc.edu/lumen/MedEd/softchalkhdht/ CMEFacDevWebPage/Plan.gif
- http://www.caneval.com/vision/venturing.html

REGISTER

This book for more content

(Audios, Special Reports, etc.)

at:

BrandtoSellBook.com

www.ingramcontent.com/pod-product-compliance
Lightning Source LLC
Chambersburg PA
CBHW060529210326
41519CB00014B/3174